The Myth of the 200 Barrier

How to Lead through Transitional Growth

Kevin E. Martin

ABINGDON PRESS
NASHVILLE

THE MYTH OF THE 200 BARRIER
HOW TO LEAD THROUGH TRANSITIONAL GROWTH

Copyright © 2005 by Abingdon Press

Library of Congress Cataloging-in-Publication Data

Martin, Kevin E., 1946-
    The myth of the 200 barrier : how to lead through transitional growth / Kevin E. Martin.
        p. cm.
    Includes bibliographical references.
    ISBN 0-687-34324-0 (pbk. : alk. paper)
    1. Church growth.   2. Small churches.   I. Title: Myth of the two hundred barrier. II. Title.

BV652.25.M195 2005
254'.5—dc22

2005009565

06 07 08 09 10 11 12 13 14—10 9 8 7 6 5 4 3
MANUFACTURED IN THE UNITED STATES OF AMERICA

Contents

Introduction

Why is it so hard to grow a small congregation into a large one? This question is at the core of this book. The overwhelming evidence is that it is very hard to take an existing small congregation and lead it to substantial growth. This has proved to be so consistently true that the idea of a 200 Barrier has emerged as a standard belief among many church leaders. This concept of the 200 Barrier states that there is a predictable barrier when Sunday attendance nears 200 that a congregation must break through in order to grow. Books and conferences have been written on this topic for many years now.

Although I agree that it is difficult to grow a small church into a large one, I do not believe that the idea of a barrier helps pastors and lay leaders develop their congregations. The barrier idea causes us to use the wrong model for congregational development and to take on shortsighted strategies detached from a more systematic approach. We are now living in a whole new generation of congregational development thinking that gives us better tools in understanding how congregations work. We need to apply this information to the task of growing a small church into a larger one.

As my mentor and teacher over the years, Lyle Schaller, contends, there is a difference between small churches and large churches. This difference is more than style or numbers. It is a difference in "what church is like around here!" So, to grow a small church into a large one is to transform the very culture of the congregation.

There are some congregations that are caught between the typical size of a small church and the necessary size of larger churches. This is what I call the "transitional size" congregation. Although not a true church size, transitional congregations share many things in common. They are high-stressed congregations that need to either get smaller or larger to be able to function more effectively.

When I first became the congregational development officer for a large Episcopal diocese, I already knew something about transitional churches. I learned over the next few years that with help these congregations could not only make the transition to a larger size but could continue to build on this transition to become very large congregations.

During my ten years in the Diocese of Texas, we were the fastest growing judicatory in our denomination. The centerpiece of our strategy was to invest heavily in two types of congregations. One was the new church plant. The other type was the church averaging between 140 and 225 in attendance, our transitional congregations. What I learned from working with these congregations is the content of this book.

I am deeply indebted to the Right Reverend Claude Payne, bishop of Texas, now retired, for his support. In my time there, the staff of the diocese was an extraordinary team. I also owe much to the clergy and lay leaders of Texas who taught me so much. I have been privileged to share information with a group of denominational "champions" called together by Dave Travis of Leadership Network.

I have tried to base this book on good congregational theory that has been proved in the soil of real congregations. I believe that pastors of small congregations will find this information helpful in creating realistic expectations for their work. I especially hope that pastors of transitional size congregations will be able to capitalize on this information and plan a hopeful and growing future for their congregations.

Kevin E. Martin

Part One

Understanding
Congregational Culture

Chapter 1

Large or Small?

Since the mid-1960s, one trend has dominated congregational life in America. This trend affects every congregation, and all leaders—lay and ordained—should be aware of it. Simply stated it is this: *Large congregations are getting larger and small congregations tend to remain the same or get smaller!*

This is, of course, the general trend and there are notable exceptions. Some extraordinary leaders in smaller congregations have offset this trend. Some large congregations have suffered reversals and become smaller. However, this trend still dominates the approximately 325,000 Protestant congregations in North America.

When I share this information with congregational leaders, they are quick to ask why. I tell them that this is actually the second question to ask. The more essential question for any congregational leader is, "What is large?" What measurement would we use to determine if a congregation is a large church or a small one? Put another way, are you helping lead a small congregation against the odds or are you trying to lead a large congregation that is trying to figure out how to ride this trend toward growth? What is large and what is small? And what is the dividing point?

Many leaders are surprised to discover that the dividing line is 150 in average attendance on Sunday mornings. In his recent book *Small Congregation Big Potential*, Lyle Schaller presents a strong argument why the dividing line should be set at 150. He points out that there is strong statistical evidence to support this number.

Why would we use average Sunday attendance to

determine this? Those who study congregations know that the Average Sunday Attendance (or ASA) is a much better measurement of congregational size than membership. Membership numbers are often deceptive. Many congregations carry members on their rolls long after these people have withdrawn from the congregation. In addition, many denominations define membership in very different ways. The ASA is the total of all people, adults and children, present on Sunday mornings for the year, divided by 52. This gives a very stable number, and tracking this number over several years shows a congregation's trend.

There is one additional part of this trend that we should note. While, generally speaking, small congregations get smaller, the opposite holds true for larger congregations. For them, the more their ASA is above 150, the greater the chance that they will grow. In today's world, size is an advantage. Contrary to popular belief, today it is easier to pastor a congregation with an ASA of 500 than to pastor a congregation with an ASA of 140. This is so counterintuitive that many clergy, denominational leaders, and lay boards cannot grasp this trend and its consequences. For example, this trend accounts for much of the decline of the once called "mainline churches" of America. Most of these denominational churches have an ASA below 150. For example, in my denomination, the Episcopal Church, the average Sunday attendance is 125, but the median attendance is around 80.

I want to make it clear that by pointing out this trend I am not making a comment on the "quality" of a congregation's life based on its size. There is nothing particularly virtuous in having a congregation with an ASA of 500 versus one with 145. There are wonderful examples of faithful, disciple-making, deeply committed congregations in smaller sizes. There can be little doubt, however, that size has a definite advantage in American culture today.

Knowing this trend and what makes for small and large congregations, we are now ready to address the second question, "Why?" To get at the reasons for this trend, we must remember that congregations are social communities that exist in the wider culture. What happens in the culture happens to congregations. Changes in the culture since the 1960s have produced the trends mentioned above. Without a doubt, the major change is the one brought by the maturing of the post–World War II baby-boom generation.

The Rise of Boomers

I was born on August 30, 1946. I am an old boomer. When I was graduated from a small high school in a town 17 miles north of Dallas, Texas, there were 64 seniors in my class. The next year some 120 seniors were graduated. Within five years of my graduation, the senior class numbered nearly 800. Older boomers feel as though we have spent our whole lives at the front of a thundering herd. The large number of boomers, combined with the radically different world of postwar America, produced a generation as different from their parents as any generation ever recorded. This "nontraditional" generation has changed every institution that we have touched, and the church is no exception to this. Here are some boomer trends that directly affect congregational life.

Boomers arrived in large numbers and consequently learned to live with large organizations. For boomers, larger is usually better, but more important, if a group of boomers does something, it happens in large numbers!

- **For example, several years ago while living in the Denver area, I changed my car radio to a "young country" station. Three months later, I discovered in the Denver newspaper that "young country" was the fastest growing form of radio station in America. We older boomers never know if we are trend starters or followers. Strangely, boomers believe that we are unique and nontraditional, but every time we step out**

in a new area, a large group follows. I call this the "boomer paradox."

Boomers learned to thrive on options. When people reared during the Great Depression went to school, they had few social groups from which to choose and a fairly small number of vocational alternatives. With boomers came choice. Our large numbers drove schools and other social organizations to learn the skill of providing options.

- **When I arrived as a freshman at Lewisville High School, there were only three social groups for boys. I could play a musical instrument in the band, join the Future Farmers of America, or play sports. Soon afterward, the subgroups in American high schools became so complex that they rival many small nation-states.**

Boomers are the first TV generation. We are more visually oriented than our parents. Further, we are accustomed to receiving information at a faster pace through various styles of communication.

- **Many Protestant churches have been very slow to respond to this change in processing information. Many American congregations continue with a nineteenth-century pace of slowly delivered oral communication.**

Boomers have eclectic tastes in music and demand that music be presented in high quality. Needless to say, high-quality music is not as highly valued, and often not an option, for most small congregations.

- **Many adults under 40 years of age have never heard a vinyl record and have been reared listening to CDs and digitally enhanced recordings.**

Boomers are nontraditional when it comes to organizations. We demand participation. Boomers consider any decision, no matter how good, made without our input, as bad. Boomers are behind the movement from representative democracy to participatory democracy.

- **This trend is transforming all the institutions of our society. Gone are the decisions made by an elite group of people in smoke-filled rooms. Today, most leaders have learned that the process of decision making is as important as the decision itself.**

Boomers started the trend of breaking with organizational and institutional loyalty. In 1950, only 4 percent of a denomination's members were once members of another denomination. Today this number is well over 50 percent and many adults have been members of several different denominational groups during their lifetimes.

- **In the future, congregations will learn the wisdom of creating "associate membership" for those who participate in other congregations and do not want to limit their memberships to just one congregation.**

Other Factors Driving Congregational Size

Although boomers account for much of the congregational trends, a few other factors should also be noted. Among these I would list:

- *The growth of electronic music and the use of CDs.* Digitally enhanced music has created an expectation of "excellence" that few small churches can produce.
- *The growth of technology.* The younger people are, the more naturally they see technology as a part of

their world. This means that technology can fit alongside worship and not be seen as a work of the devil.

- *The rise of the large city that matched the movement away from rural communities and towns.* The twentieth century has been one of migration away from farms and towns and toward large urban areas. This gives urban congregations large numbers of nonchurched and newly arrived populations from which to draw.
- *The rapidly changing forms of oral communication.* This has tended to benefit pastors in larger congregations. Hence, the contemporary large-church pastor tends to preach with no pulpit while his image is interspersed with his "points" and quotations on a large screen.
- *The growing trend away from professionals to "how-to," hands-on, and participatory ways of working.* Just check out cable TV and its multiple how-to programs ranging from tiling your kitchen to the latest techniques in surgery.

All these factors benefit larger congregations and work against smaller congregations. Is it possible to have a dynamic and healthy congregation with fewer than 150 people attending on an average Sunday? Yes. But today, leaders of smaller congregations must work harder than ever to have this happen.

Perhaps the best analogy is found in medicine. Many years ago, the family doctor was a generalist who treated the whole family. He needed to know a little about most illnesses and enough to diagnose and treat people. Then came specialization. However, specialization has also brought us the "family medicine practitioner." This doctor is a specialist, not a generalist. Those of us who work with pastors know that the pastor of the congregation with 75 to 150 people attending on a Sunday is now serving in a highly specialized calling. The generalist pastor, who loved the people, preached sermons, and ran a denominationally based Sunday school, has now retired or should do so immediately.

The cultural pressures that push small congregations smaller and larger ones larger has created a critical problem for the congregation that numbers between 150 and 225 attendees. The common experience of these problems has given rise to the belief that growing congregations tend to hit a barrier. We will take a closer look in the next chapter at whether or not there is a barrier.

Questions

1. How large is your congregation? (To determine this, plot two lines on a graph. Line one should be the average attendance for the past ten years. Line two should be the number of pledging units—or giving units—for the same period.)

2. How long has your congregation been this size?

3. What is the current trend?

4. Based on an ASA of 150, is your congregation large or small?

Large or Small?

Chapter 2

Hitting the 200 Barrier?

When Pastor John James came to First Church, he was told by his denominational executive that this congregation, located in a growing suburb, had "never really gotten off the ground." First Church had been started 18 years earlier by a group of families from the downtown denominational congregation. With the support of the denomination, these families began holding Sunday services in a funeral home. Their first pastor was a schoolteacher from a neighboring community. He served the congregation for four years. Then the congregation called its first full-time pastor.

Under the direction this first full-time pastor, First Church grew from an ASA of around 50 to almost 100. During this time, they built a lovely white-frame church with a spire topped with a cross. This building was built to seat 125 in anticipation of further growth. After serving faithfully for a long tenure, their pastor was called to a much larger congregation. After eight months of seeking, First Church found a young and energetic female pastor. Although some families left because of the new pastor's gender, several new families arrived, and by her fourth year the ASA of First Church had risen to almost 120. Unfortunately for First Church, their pastor was soon called to teach pastoral care at the denomination's seminary.

Then came trouble. First Church called a 48-year-old pastor with a track record of growing his previous congregation. Shortly after he arrived, the pastor announced that his wife had decided to move back to their previous town and that she wanted a divorce. For the next three years, the pastor struggled with a number of personal issues. For many months he was clearly depressed. Fortunately for the church, their pastor's depression finally lifted. Soon after, he fell in love with and married a woman he had met at a Christian education conference. At first, the members of the congregation seemed to welcome his new bride, but then their pastor recommended that she be given a paid position as the Christian education staff person. This led to open conflict because she was replacing a long-standing and beloved volunteer. After seven months of angry board meetings and dissatisfaction, the pastor resigned. The ASA for his last year was 93.

It was two years before First Church called Pastor James. During the interim, the congregation was served by a series of bivocational clergy. When Pastor James arrived, the ASA had dropped to 78. Meanwhile the suburban community around First Church had continued to grow. From every indication, the denominational executive was right; First Church had never reached its potential. It also seemed clear to the members that what they really needed was a pastor with the kind of energy that their first full-time clergy person possessed.

Pastor James's first few years at First Church were full of activities and growth. The congregation built its fellowship hall and expanded rooms for Sunday school. Pastor James introduced a midweek multigeneration education program. By his third year, First Church had filled its church building. Their ASA was over 125 and most Sundays they had to set up extra chairs.

To accommodate the rapid growth, the board followed Pastor James's advice and started a second service. For years they had a 10 A.M. service followed by Sunday school. Now they added an 8:30 A.M. service for young families followed by Sunday school for all ages. A more traditional 10:45 A.M. service followed with a "children's chapel" during the sermon time. Since Pastor James was both an effective preacher and good Bible teacher, he offered a 10 A.M. adult education class. This soon filled the fellowship hall. By the end of his fifth year, ASA had risen to 165. First Church seemed destined to finally reach its potential!

By his eighth year as pastor, First Church had reached an ASA of 193. The next year it dropped back to 182. At the recommendation of a fellow clergy person, Pastor James attended a denominational conference on "Breaking the 200 Barrier." Everything he learned there seemed to make sense. His congregation had hit a predictable barrier right around an ASA of 200. He returned from the seminar with three new strategies he wanted to pursue to help First Church break through this barrier.

Attempting to Break the Barrier

First, he introduced the idea of home fellowships. Within the next year he had four up and running. These were weekly fellowship groups that met for mutual support and Bible study. Pastor James prepared the outlines for each week's study and discussion. He met regularly with the home fellowship leaders to train them and support their work.

Next, he added two additional Sunday morning adult education classes. Both used a more informal discussion format and offered an alternative to Pastor James's lecture method. Both classes leveled out quickly at fewer than a dozen participants. This did little to solve the crowding problem in the fellowship hall.

Finally, Pastor James overcame considerable resistance and convinced his board to hire their Christian education person on a full-time basis. Although she was a beloved member and active volunteer, First Church had never offered to pay her before. Confronted with the growing number of hours she now was serving a week, the board finally agreed to pay her.

Pastor James finished his tenth year with a real sense of satisfaction. The church had never seemed busier. There were more opportunities from which new families could choose. The church buildings were full each Sunday. Easter attendance that year had reached a record 387 people. Even so, Pastor James was stunned to discover that the ASA of the congregation had only risen from the previous 182 to 186! He began to realize that it just might not be possible for First Church to break the 200 Barrier, especially with him as pastor.

He began to feel that his hands-on style of relational leadership must be holding the congregation back. He began to realize that he could not seem to make the transition from shepherd of the sheep to rancher of a larger organization—an image used in the conference he had attended. More and more, the potential of this congregation began to become a point of judgment on his leadership. No matter how much he tried to conceive of himself as a rancher, all his instincts were for personal, hands-on contact with people. When he tried to conceive of a church where he was detached from many of the activities and ministries, he resisted the image. He also inwardly worried if his style of pastoring meant that he would be limited to serving only smaller congregations. He intuitively felt that he could manage a larger congregation. He knew many pastors in his denomination who led larger congregations, and he felt that he was as capable as they. This entire shepherd versus rancher business began to confuse him.

The next year he received a call to serve a 650 ASA congregation in the next state. This created a real dilemma for Pastor James. He loved First Church. He had given a great deal of his best years to this congregation. However, his children were approaching college age and he could use the considerable salary increase the larger congregation offered him for college expenses. Most of all, as hard as he had worked the past two years, he knew that he simply wasn't up to another run at the 200 Barrier. Of course, he did have some inner doubts as to whether he was capable of running the larger congregation since he seemed to have limits on being able to grow First Church. What finally convinced him to make the move was the presence of so many capable staff members in this larger church. Pastor James knew that whatever his limitations as a leader, he would have help in running this larger congregation.

The year after Pastor James left, the ASA dropped to 163. By the end of his successor's first year, it dropped to 145.

When Pastor James learned about how his former congregation was doing, he had mixed feelings. On the one hand, he was sad that things did not seem to be going well for his successor. On the other hand, he was secretly relieved that the new pastor had not suddenly broken the 200 Barrier. He felt confirmed that the issues had not been all his fault, but that First Church just was not capable of breaking an ASA of 200.

This example seems to confirm the idea of a 200 Barrier. The image of this barrier has become a popular one among American pastors. For many years, the Fuller Church Growth Institute ran a seminar on breaking the 200 Barrier. Because there are so many smaller congregations, thousands of pastors attended this seminar, determined to lead their congregations to growth. Books have even been written on "the church growth pastor" who is able to break through this barrier. Yet, the overwhelming evidence is that few smaller churches make the transition into the larger size. Does this confirm the existence of such a barrier, or does it demonstrate that the model that proposes such a barrier simply doesn't work? This is what I have come to learn, namely that the 200 Barrier is a myth. In the next chapter, we will explore this myth further and discover a different way of seeing the problem of helping a small church become a large one.

Questions

1. What elements of Pastor James's story seem to confirm the belief that there is a barrier?

2. What other elements do you see affecting the size of the congregation besides the efforts of the pastor?

3. Why do you think Pastor James could lead a much larger church, but did not seem able to break through the 200 Barrier of First Church?

Chapter 3

The Myth of the 200 Barrier

During the last 20 years, thousands of pastors across America have attended seminars and workshops intended to help them break the 200 Barrier. Interestingly, studies have shown that a very small percentage of congregations that have sent pastors to these seminars have ever broken this barrier. Supporters of the 200 Barrier idea point to this as proof that the barrier does exist. Most pastors, like Pastor James, no matter how gifted, ever lead a congregation beyond this barrier.

The example in the previous chapter may seem to confirm the idea of the 200 Barrier, but my experience is that the 200 Barrier is a myth. In addition, it is also a myth that becomes a self-fulfilling prophecy. As pastors make adjustments to their congregation to prepare to break this barrier, they often find that decline rather than growth follow these adjustments.

People who believe in the 200 Barrier believe that this barrier can only be broken by two strategies. Some teach one of them, some both. These strategies can be described as follows.

Strategy One: From Shepherd to Rancher

This theory holds that to break the 200 Barrier the pastor must change his or her "style" of ministry. The pastor of a smaller church is like a shepherd, whose style is one-on-one and personal. This pastor has read too much of the Gospel of John with its admonition that "the sheep hear [the shepherd's] voice.... They will not follow a stranger" (John 10:3), and wants to know all the sheep by name and to minister to each personally. This style of pastoral leadership is inadequate to break the 200 Barrier. To break through, such a pastor must learn that the pastor of a large congregation is more like a rancher than a shepherd.

The rancher doesn't just have sheep, the rancher also has cattle, crops, oil wells, and even a specialty sheep enterprise. The rancher flies about the ranch in a helicopter visiting each of these endeavors and managing the total operation. The rancher has ranch hands (staff) who manage each of the individual areas of the ranch's operations. This theory believes that teaching shepherds to be ranchers is the way to break this barrier. Whereas the shepherd is obviously a hands-on deliverer of services, the rancher is a manager of an organization.

Strategy Two: From Relationships to Programs

This theory notes that larger congregations have extensive programs and that these programs are very different from the kinds of groups and ministries smaller congregations have. The secret to breaking the barrier is to institute one or more of these programs.

One program, the small group or cell, has been a favorite for the past several years. Christian bookstores have numerous books on creating small-group ministries. A favorite mantra of those who promote this theory is that "you grow larger by growing smaller." By creating a small-group system and then multiplying the number of small groups, the congregation will take off.

What is the task of such small groups? I have found that each author and exponent of small groups believes strongly that their type of small group is the best. Some small groups are created to meet the pastoral and intimacy needs of new generations. Some small groups are intended to build up

Christians in their knowledge of the scriptures. Some are aimed at prayer. Some are clearly disciple-making groups intended to deepen an individual's growth in following the Lord. Some are evangelistic, intended to lead others to Christ.

Whatever the theme, the thesis is essentially the same. First, this is the type of small group your congregation needs. Second, multiply these and your congregation will grow. There are, of course, outstanding examples of congregations that have used the cell-group model to grow at amazing rates. These examples are often pointed to as proof. A better question would focus our attention on the thousands of congregations that have attempted the cell-group method and failed to see the congregation grow. A closely related issue is the number of congregations that have found that it takes at least three major efforts at forming small groups for them to get off the ground. Even having gotten off the ground, such groups may not necessarily lead the congregation to major growth.

Some authors recommend a combination of these strategies. These authors argue that it is not either one of these that is important in growth, but a combination of the two. The argument is that a change in management style combined with a right programmatic approach will crash the congregation through the barrier and on to growth. So there it sits, this barrier. The congregation is envisioned as a moving vehicle that needs mass and momentum to crash beyond it.

When I consult with clergy who lead congregations around the 150 ASA mark, I find that they frequently ask, "What program would you recommend to help us break through the 200 Barrier?" My answer is, "What barrier is that?" I then explain that they are asking the wrong question. The first question should be, "What has made this a successful and growing pastoral church?" The second question should be, "How will I need to transform the present culture to allow the congregation to grow to a larger size?"

Understanding the System

There is a much more comprehensive way to understand congregational development. It, too, is rooted in research on congregational size and it, too, is illustrated by looking at the ASA of congregations. Let's revisit the research for a moment to look at congregations as systems rather than organizations.

If you randomly chose a sampling of 1,000 congregations, you would discover an interesting fact about their ASA. Let's say the smallest congregation has an ASA of eight, and the largest has 2,650. Imagine a line from the smallest to largest that represents a continuum of these churches.

8 _____ 2,650

If you make a graph with each congregation on it, you will make some interesting discoveries. One such discovery was made 40 years ago. It is that the two most predictable patterns of statistical disbursement don't hold up. What are these?

First, statistically you could expect that the 1,000 congregations would be distributed "randomly" across the spectrum. This was not what researchers found. This was not too surprising because any casual look at congregations suggested to the observer that there are many more smaller congregations than larger ones.

Second, and more predictably, you would expect the dots to produce a bell curve. The high point of the bell curve would be near the average of the congregations. In our example, this would be 265. In a pure bell curve distribution, the median and the average would be the same. Figure 3.1 shows what a random sampling of our congregations would look like if it followed this statistical pattern.

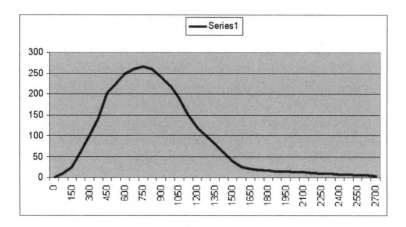

Figure 3.1
Random sampling of congregations
using a pure bell curve model.

A pure bell curve distribution is not what researchers found. There wasn't a random pattern or a bell curve. What they did find revolutionized the way that we understand congregations. There was not one bell curve. There were several bell curves! Congregations tended to cluster around certain predictable numbers.

It is very important to remember that this has nothing to do with a congregation's denominational affiliation or its location. Researchers knew that there must be a reason for these clusters. Armed with this information, they returned to these various bell curves with a second set of questions. Here is a brief summary of the essential findings that have unfolded over the years.

Congregational Distribution

There are a number of congregations in a bell curve at the low end of the scale that represents a strong cluster of congregations with an ASA of around 20 to 45 people. This group represents the cluster with the largest number of congregations. In studying this group, it was found that these congregations are made up of extended family groupings and are often served by part-time or bivocational clergy. These congregations are now generally called "family size churches." They have a very predictable nature and style.

A second large bell curve, slightly higher up, is centered around an ASA of 110. These congregations are also very predictable in style. They are usually made up of a group of 60 to 80 households who support the services of a full-time pastor and have an ASA between 76 and 140. These congregations are now called "pastoral size churches."

Further up the scale between 225 and 400 is a smaller cluster of congregations now called "program size churches." Actually, "small program size churches" is a more accurate title because there are several smaller clusters farther up the scale. It is very important to note that whereas the largest numbers of churches are found in the first two clusters—family and pastoral—most members are found in the clusters above 225. As one accountant explained, "Larger numbers add up faster than smaller numbers!"

Church Sizes and Types

The Family Size: 3 to 75 ASA with a median of 35
These congregations function as extended families and are usually served by bivocational clergy.

The Pastoral Size: 76 to 140 ASA with a median of 110
These congregations are organized around the support of a full-time pastor. They tend to have 60 to 80 active families, primarily parents and their children.

The Small Program Size: 225 to 400 ASA
In these congregations staff have emerged as important

leaders and the congregation has developed programs beyond worship and Christian education, often felt-need ministries.

The Medium Program Size: 400 to 600 ASA
These congregations tend to be strong in staff, program, and stewardship while still maintaining a high percentage of members who attend each Sunday.

The Large Program Size: 600 to 900 ASA
The staff and program leaders of this size church look much like the extended family of the smaller family-size church. The quality of teamwork in the large-program size church often sets the tone for the rest of the church.

The Corporate Size: 1000+ ASA
This is the true large church in America. Often, oversight of the staff is delegated to associate clergy, freeing up the senior pastor primarily for preaching, teaching, and vision casting.

This distribution pattern means that there is a difference between the median congregation and the average congregation. In my denomination, the Episcopal Church, most congregations have an ASA of 125, but the median is 79. For United Methodists, the median is 40. When the median is much lower than the average, the statistics reveal this truth: There are many more small congregations than larger ones; however, there are more people in the larger congregations than the smaller ones! This is true of almost all mainline denominations in this country.

An important side issue revealed by this information is worth mentioning. The large number of smaller congregations tells us why most judicatories are captivated (some would say held hostage) by their smaller congregations. In most denominations, small churches are overrepresented in their decision-making bodies.

The Myth of the 200 Barrier

When I became the congregational development officer for an Episcopal diocese with 157 congregations, about one-third (51) of our congregations had fewer than 75 people attending on a Sunday. These churches had only 7 percent of our membership. Meanwhile, 14 of our congregations had more than 400 attending on a Sunday and contained more than 35 percent of our membership.

What does all this research tell us? It tells us that there are predictable ways of being a church. These ways of being a church have predictable characteristics. We now know that each of these sizes represents a predictable "system." Each system has elements that bring energy, life, and growth. The system also has elements that keep the system from becoming too large. In systems theory, elements that bring energy to a system are called "reinforcers," whereas those that contain energy are called "balancers." These two types of elements keep the system within certain boundaries.

Of course, most laypeople do not talk about their church's system. They just talk about "the way things are around here." In other words, each system has a reinforcing style that is characteristic of that size and that produces a congregational culture. I believe that is it natural for human beings to bring to our systems and organizations predictability. It is this culture or predictability that makes transforming a small congregation into a larger one so difficult. Obviously, the longer a congregation has operated within a particular size, the more established in the DNA of the congregation is this expectation. Many congregational development people believe that a congregation's size is imprinted in its first 30 years of existence. After this first development period, changing this DNA becomes very difficult.

Rather than thinking of a barrier out there, it would be better to ask, "How large can a small church be and still retain the culture of a small church?" I believe the answer to this question is between 125 and 150 ASA. There are elements that can push the pastoral size church above 150 ASA, but, over time, the culture will work to bring it back to a more workable and predictable place. In a later chapter, I will point out how churches between 150 and 225 ASA are "anxious systems" that are highly vulnerable to change. Before we move on, however, there is another dynamic of size that we need to acknowledge. This has to do with healthy and unhealthy systems.

Healthy and Unhealthy Systems

A system can be healthy or unhealthy. When the system is healthy, it most predictably produces an ASA in the middle of the bell curve or cluster. This understanding is beginning to revolutionize congregational development. It has overwhelming implications for church planting, evangelism, leadership development, seminary education, and denominational strategies.

A fundamental issue for many small congregations is health, not growth. Many smaller American congregations do not incorporate new members and make new disciples for Jesus Christ well because their system is an unhealthy one. This does not mean that the system does not work. Indeed, the system still functions. Its boundaries stay in place. However, the system survives in unhealthy ways. Put another way, we can say it exists for the maintenance of the system as an end in itself.

These systems need leaders who are first capable of bringing health to the church before growth can be a goal. Some growth efforts are merely efforts to mask the dysfunction of a congregation. They create more anxiety that feeds an already unhealthy system.

For many small congregations, I recommend a brief but important assessment tool. I suggest that leaders create a scale from one to ten. This scale measures the congregation's self-esteem. If a leader scored a congregation as a one, he or she would be saying, "I am not sure why I even bother to attend here." On the ten side of the scale, the leader is saying, "This is one of the best caring, loving, and Christian communities in this country!" I then average the score of the leaders. I have consistently found that a church whose leaders score it below five is in decline. A church where leaders score it as above six is almost always growing.

Curiously, leaders are often very loyal and committed to their congregations even when they score them low on the scale. These congregations function like an alcoholic family. Members of the family may love one another and remain loyal, but they will tend to isolate the family and not invite strangers into it. The low-esteem congregation is often poor at inviting others into the church family.

• The Healthy System Checklist •

In order to keep your congregation healthy and functional, review the following items. Place a "Y" by each item that you already have and an "N" by those you do not.

_____ 1. We rotate members of the vestry on a three-year basis; off-going members must leave the vestry for one year before being reelected.

_____ 2. We rotate officers of the congregation (clerk, treasurer, etc.) just as we do vestry members, not allowing them to serve more than five years in one office.

_____ 3. We do not allow members of the same family to serve the vestry at the same time.

_____ 4. We provide training for leaders suitable to their office.

_____ 5. We participate in training events available beyond our local congregation.

_____ 6. We utilize an open communication system and we actively seek feedback from members, especially new ones.

_____ 7. We delegate decision making in appropriate ways beyond the vestry. We encourage committees, commissions, and other work groups to be responsible for aspects of the congregation's life beyond the vestry.

_____ 8. We have a workable mission statement and a list of present goals.

_____ 9. We hold an annual meeting (if possible in a retreat setting) to review our current goals and to plan for the future.

_____ 10. We hold an active annual stewardship program in which all members are encouraged to support the congregation financially and to express feedback about the nature and degree of their support.

_____ 11. We have an active assimilation plan for new members. We quickly recruit them to vital areas of our congregation's life.

_____ 12. We have in place a means of responding to conflict, bringing it to healthy resolve and reconciliation between members when necessary.

Two Types of Growth

Understanding congregational culture and the boundaries around these sizes also helps us understand something about congregational growth. There are actually two kinds of growth.

- Growth within the boundaries of a system is congruent growth. It is consistent with the community's self-perception and culture.

- Growth beyond the boundaries of a system is transformational growth. This is growth that is not consistent with the present system.

When smaller churches think of growth, the leaders are thinking of congruent growth. Most are not thinking of transformational growth. My experience is that most leaders of smaller congregations that are looking for a new pastor want someone who will bring congruent growth, not transformational growth. The pastoral size church growing from 90 to 110 tends to feel good about the growth. This growth reinforces the congregation's self-image and builds its esteem. Usually, such growth happens because the church is getting better at being a pastoral church. This kind of growth usually does not bring stress to the congregation.

I have found that most pastors are trained by their denominational systems to be conventional leaders of the present systems. Few pastors are ever given the information that might allow them to be transformational leaders. Many of us in the congregational development field have come to believe that the whole purpose of seminary training is to acculturate future clergy to our present system. Indeed, discernment committees frequently reject candidates with strong transformational and growth leadership skills. Needless to say, these realities make it very difficult for mainline denominations to find both transformational leaders and church planters.

The Myth and the Reality

All this also explains to us why the 200 Barrier is a myth. A better model is to understand that few pastoral size congregations can sustain more than 200 people on an average Sunday. It is beyond the system's capacity. There was a time when ethnic homogeny in a community would allow one pastor to lead a very large church in a purely pastoral style; the Herr Pastor of the Lutheran tradition, for example. Today, the complexity of modern society has changed this.

Therefore, to grow beyond the 200 number demands a systemic change. True, this could involve a shift in the pastor's leadership style and it will demand the creation of programs. However, these are only parts of a different way of being church; a different system. At the core, it will demand a change in the mind-set of the congregational members. It will need to start with the pastor and the lay leadership, but eventually the general membership will have to see the congregation in a new way. Of course, even when this transformation takes place, there are always some members who continue to see the congregation as the smaller church they initially joined. After all, congregational culture is hard to change because people are hard to change.

In part 2, we will look at three types of congregations and how these three—the pastoral, the program, and the transitional—show us how leaders sustain and grow these congregations. We will take a look at the predictable stress points for each size and we will note the difference between congruent growth and transformational growth. Before we leave this whole business of culture and sizes, however, we will take another look at why the number 150 is so important to churches. This I call the "Rule of 150."

The Myth of the 200 Barrier

Questions

1. What assumptions about "the way church is around here" do your people make?

2. What tensions would occur if suddenly attendance in your congregation dropped by half?

3. What if attendance suddenly doubled?

Chapter 4

The Rule of 150

What is the Rule of 150 and how does it apply to our conversation about congregational culture and sizes? I discovered the Rule of 150 in reading Malcolm Gladwell's book *The Tipping Point*. This book is about how little things can often make a big difference. Gladwell takes a look at a number of large movements from the sudden revitalized sales of Hush Puppies in 1992 to the sudden drop in crime rates in New York City in the 1990s. The book is an interesting read on many levels, but I had to stop and take notes when I came across the Rule of 150.

The Rule of 150 caught my attention because it answered a question that I have often wrestled with as a consultant. Why do certain numbers seem to be so predictable? For example, why do pastoral size churches that seem to be so stable and healthy at 125 attendees per Sunday become so unstable as the number moves toward 150?

It was this predictability that helped me set the number 140 as the top number for the pastoral church and the beginning point for the transitional church, which numbers from 141 to 225 attendees. Again, the transitional church isn't a true congregational culture, it represents the gap that exists between two very predictable types of churches, the pastoral and program.

My intuitive explanation was that at 125 a congregation begins to grow beyond the ability of the pastor to meet the needs of a certain number of households. Although I still believe this is true, the Rule of 150 explains this in a more sophisticated and scientific way.

Gladwell starts with a common explanation of the

complexity of relationships. For example, if you are in a group of four people, you have six relationships to track, yours plus the other three people's relationships to one another.

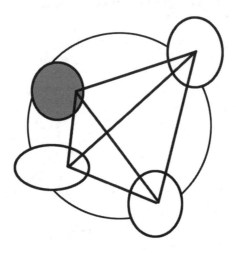

However, if the group grows to 14, you now have 92 relationships to track! The relationships grow exponentially.

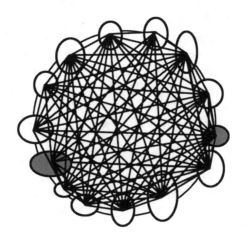

So, at what point does a group become too large for us to manage all the relationships? Gladwell thinks that fewer than 12 is the best size and that 12 to 15 relationships is the point where the complexity makes close relationships difficult.

This begins to explain the upper limits of the pastoral church because the typical one has about 15 leadership roles. As the number extends beyond 12, the church begins to reach some natural limits found in the leadership core. This means that the typical pastor must work well with 15 elected and appointed leaders. This also explains why the effective small group has fewer than 12 members.

Then Gladwell asks, if there is a maximum number of social relationships among people? In other words, if 15 is *my* maximum number, what is *our* maximum number? As it turns out, there has been some interesting research on this very question. British anthropologist Robin Dunbar did extensive investigation on this topic. He measured the neocortex of primates and their typical group size. You may remember that the human brain is the largest of all primates. Dunbar found a direct relationship between brain size and the social size of groups. He set the human number at just over 147.

Dunbar then studied 21 tribal peoples worldwide to test his number. What he discovered was remarkable. The average size of a tribal group was just over 148! This led Dunbar to formulate the Rule of 150. Briefly, this rule states that at 150, the number of relationships among people becomes so complex that the group must either divide or face social disintegration.

Now let me translate the Rule of 150 into congregational language. A longtime member of a now growing pastoral church approaches the pastor with these words, "My wife and I are thinking of leaving because this just isn't the same congregation that we joined 15 years ago." Another typical example is, "I once knew everyone in this church, now we have grown so large that I hardly recognize anyone." Both these comments, heard in transitional congregations, reflect the personal experience of social overcomplexity.

How, then, is a large church able to be large? By either having more than one social group or by having a great many small groups. Actually, I believe it is an artful combination of the two. For example, in a program church with nine staff members, some staff members are managing a subcongregation that could grow to 150 people. However, the pastor has to manage the small group called the staff. I believe that the healthy large church has learned the art of managing the interaction between these two numbers of 12 and 150.

In a way, what I am suggesting is that congregational growth and interaction demand the artful management of two sets of numbers—12 and 150. A healthy congregation will pay attention to the number of groups that run between 6 and 12 members. Whenever this size exceeds 12, the pastor can anticipate problems. The number 150 works the same. Whenever a service or group exceeds 150 members, problems or tension will develop. Even a very large congregation with attendance around 1,000 is actually made up of combinations of these smaller numbers.

However we view a congregation, the Rule of 150 reinforces why the demarcation line in America between large and small churches is 150. With this reinforcement, we are ready to take a look at pastors and styles of leadership and how these relate to the growth of a small church into a large one.

Questions

1. What does the Rule of 12 say about your present groups in your church?

2. How does the limit of 150 apply to your various worship services and ministries?

3. How well does your congregation manage these different size groups?

Part Two

Three Types of Congregations

Chapter 5

The Pastoral Size Congregation

For hundreds of years following the Protestant Reformation, the pastoral size congregation has dominated the religious maps of Europe and North America. This form of religious community worked effectively. As new communities were settled in the New World, this pattern was easily reproduced. For example, newly arrived German immigrants could associate together and call a pastor. This pastor helped provide stability and pastoral support to the families.

This pastor and his family lived among the people, loved them, baptized them, married them, encouraged them, scolded them, and finally buried them. This pastor did provide pastoral care to these families, but, without a doubt, the primary role of this pastor was to teach the faith of the parents to their children. In England, the parish parson was often one of the few educated people in the village. In the seventeenth through the nineteenth centuries, the parson's sermons provided entertainment, education, and community cohesiveness.

When there was ethnic, social, or political homogeneity, the pastor had charge of the whole community and all its families. As society diversified and other denominations came to the community, the glue of the community was represented by the pastor's ability to connect to the families. This gives us the key to the boundaries and numbers that exist in this system. The average person can track somewhere between 60 and 80 households. If these families give financially to support the congregation, they can provide for the pastor and his family on the normative level of the local families. We will see later how today's economy works against the pastoral size congregation, although the system worked for decades.

If we notice the relationship of the pastor to the number of households, we learn several characteristics of the pastoral church.

- If the congregation has large families, as in rural or suburban communities, the 60 to 80 families produce a large congregation, some numbering more than 150.
- If the congregation is in the inner city, where families are emotionally and economically stressed (add to this the number of single-parent households), the congregation could number in the 70s.
- If too many families experience stress, the pastor's ability to provide emotional attention to all the families is diminished.
- If the pastor or his family experience emotional distress, the pastor's ability to provide emotional attention to all the families is limited.
- Very important, if the energetic pastor comes to a low-number congregation and grows it by recruiting new families, this system will predictably reach its upper level—the number of households that particular pastor can track.
- When that energetic pastor leaves, the congregation will predictably decline for a period of time.

The Typical Pastoral Size Church

We are now ready to describe the typical pastoral size congregation. These are the normal characteristics. Later, we will note some exceptions. The pastoral size congregation will tend to have:

- Attendance that ranges between 76 and 140 ASA.
- Membership that tends to range between 200 and 400.
- A mailing list that tends to range between 100 and 150.
- Somewhere between 40 to 60 households who regularly give, along with another ten to 20 families who occasionally contribute.
- A leadership core made up of between 12 to 20 leadership roles.
- When healthy, the congregation will have as its two strongest generations, parents and their children.
- Most of the organizations and ministries of the congregation exist to support the needs of the community with the pastor as their leader. These ministries primarily are focused around worship and education for children.
- The pastor's calendar and the congregation's calendar are essentially the same thing.

Sometimes a pastoral size congregation becomes very large. Even though its attendance may approach 400, its life is still pastoral, centered on the personality of a particular pastor. When this talented pastor leaves, the congregation rapidly declines to the more predictable numbers. We should also note that

- pastoral churches tend to be very stable. Their ASA remains fairly constant, especially when led by the same pastor;
- the pastoral church is most at risk when it changes pastors. The normal bonding process between a new pastor and his or her congregation is about three to five years;
- a good tenure for a pastor in a pastoral sized congregation is usually between seven and 15 years;
- when a pastoral church has had a long-term pastorate of more than 15 years, the transition to a

The Pastoral Size Congregation

new pastor becomes more difficult; the longer the pastorate, the more difficult the transition. *(Pastors considering following a long-term pastorate of more than 15 years should do so with great caution. They should seek out support from their denomination and they should help the present congregational leaders be aware of the poor track record of clergy following such long-term pastorates.)*

Following the Long-term Pastorate

Why is it so difficult to follow the long-term pastor, especially those who serve longer than 15 years?

1. The congregation is normally in decline *and is most likely to continue this pattern.*

   a. There will be a predictable drop in membership, especially during the new pastor's second year.
   b. A large number of "marginal members" will use the former pastor's leaving as a time to change church attachment.
   c. A number of "historically rooted" members will feel disconnected by the former pastor's departure.

2. The departure of the former pastor will create a void *that cannot be filled by a new person.*

   a. The older the former pastor, the more likely that person functioned as a "patriarch or matriarch" and less as a leader.
   b. The earned esteem, respect, and emotional attachment that the years provided have little carryover to the new pastor.
   c. The former pastor has almost always been seen as a person of religious authority "older and more mature

than us." The new pastor could easily be younger than the average age of the church's adult members.

3. Congregations tend to make poor decisions because they are still emotionally attached to the former pastor.

> a. Most write job descriptions based on "the skills not found in our former pastor." This only accentuates the differences a new pastor brings.
> b. The longer the pastorate, the more novelty seems like a good idea. Novelty could be expressed in such areas as age, theological orientation, personal characteristics, and skill (i.e., an introvert followed by an extrovert).
> c. The grieving process for a congregation—even when people believe the former pastor has stayed too long—is three to five years. (Some long-time members may never successfully work through their grief!)

If you follow a long-tenured pastor, it is probably best to think of yourself as the interim pastor!

The Future and the Pastoral Church

There was a time when the pastor of the pastoral church was the mainstay of the mainline church. This is changing. Among the reasons for this change, we would note:

- The expanding costs to congregations of the benefits packages for a pastor, especially the cost of health care.
- The growing consumer demands of boomers that pastors be able to respond to a widening number of emotional and relational problems.
- The expanding costs of energy to keep the aging church buildings running.

- A growing competition of larger congregations better able to position themselves to meet consumer demands.
- A decreasing denominational loyalty. This means that pastors can rarely depend on denominational loyalty to make up for their inadequacies, perceived and otherwise.

Does the pastoral size congregation have a future? Yes it does, but the demands on the pastor generalist has changed immensely. Let's return to our medical analogy. When I was a child, our doctor was a medical generalist. These doctors have been replaced by family practitioners. This is now considered a specialized profession. I believe the same thing is true today of the pastor of the pastoral sized church. You have to be better prepared, better trained, and smarter than ever before.

In addition, too many pastors are learning to measure themselves by their ability to grow pastoral sized churches rather than their ability to effectively pastor them. In chapter 7 we will revisit this point. In pastoral size churches, congruent growth tends to be appreciated while transformational growth tends to be resisted. Strangely, successful programs in this size church tended to meet resistance.

Years ago, I served a pastoral size church that included a member who was active in the recovery community. She had been active in Al-Anon, a twelve-step program for the family members of people suffering with alcoholism, and had helped her husband through ten years of sobriety. With her help, we created a Wednesday-night community drug-education program. Because of her extensive contacts in the Alcoholics Anonymous and Al-Anon communities, she was able to put together a 12-week speakers program with some of the most outstanding professionals in the field. While our Sunday attendance was averaging around 125, the Wednesday-night program averaged right at 300 people for the first series.

Word of our program spread to other churches and we were inundated with requests for information on how to offer this program. We added this woman to our staff as an outreach person. I assumed that the church leaders would view this ministry as a significant success. I was caught off-guard when, at a monthly board meeting, conflict emerged. Many of our leaders resented these new people. They complained about the overuse of the facilities. They wanted to know if any of *those* people were joining our church. (In fact, they were!) They wanted assurances from me that I was attending to my regular pastoral duties and not spending too much of my time working with this group. It took several years for our leadership to accept the presence of this life-changing ministry to the community. Back then, I wondered why we had such resistance. Today, I know that this response was predictable. It was not congruent growth.

Questions

1. Who are the significant pastors you have known in your life?

2. What predictable stresses now affect pastors that weren't present 40 years ago?

3. What role does the pastor's spouse fill in the pastoral congregation?

Chapter 6

The Program Size Congregation

Congregations with an ASA of 226 to 400 have, like the pastoral size churches, a fairly predictable style and a reinforcing culture. These factors are made up of several key components. Let's take a look at these key components.

1. The Congregation Has Developed Several Ministries or Programs Aimed at Human Needs

These ministries and programs can be organized along generational lines, life stages, or other ways of serving human need. When these ministries and programs work well, they touch a felt human need that is both within the congregation and within the surrounding community.

For example, a mother's day out program can be very helpful to younger mothers struggling with the demands of raising young children. In one sense, the ministry can be successful just by measuring the number of young mothers who use the service. However, when this ministry also has members of the congregation who use the service and are active in serving other mothers, the ministry has an ability to connect the congregation to those it serves. This is the best kind of program for a larger church to offer.

Occasionally, a congregation starts a ministry such as a 12-step Christian group. The church correctly sees the need in the community, but because there are no present church members who connect to the need, the ministry does not provide a bridge to the wider community. Even if the program should become successful, some congregational leaders could come to resent the program, and even lobby for its removal.

Whereas program size churches often have large choirs and adult education programs, these are not the primary driving force of the larger congregation. It is the felt need program that best reinforces the larger churches' ministry and growth.

It is also important to note that these ministries and programs are not organized around the maintenance of a congregation. They are also not organized around denominational requirements. The men's ministry, house fellowships, the senior citizens' fellowship, and mother's day out programs are examples of these types of groups. Since the program size church has learned that not everyone has to participate in everything the church offers—a common assumption of the pastoral size church—having multiple ministries, activities, programs, and groups is seen as natural to the larger church. When these areas of ministry are functioning well, they often have a key person leading and organizing this work. This leads us to the second characteristic of such churches.

2. The Congregation Has an Organized Paid and Volunteer Staff

The size of the church, along with its emerging diversity, generates around the pastor a team of leaders specializing in congregational areas. In the smaller church, the lay board often functions in the role of both governance and operations. The complexity of the larger church makes this very difficult. The volunteer board members simply are not around enough to understand the operations of the church. Large churches, therefore, are staff-led congregations.

The presence of staff does create its own set of issues. For example, note that I mentioned both paid and volunteer staff. It would be a mistake for the pastor of larger churches to think of only the paid staff as the staff team. Since it would be very difficult for a congregation to employ people in every area of specialty, lay leaders who can give enough time to areas of ministry are important extensions of the staff of the congregation. Managing these volunteer staff people is a challenging task. Some pastors make a mistake by treating volunteer staff differently than they treat paid staff. I believe that both paid and unpaid staff should have the following:

- a clearly written job description;
- a clearly written understanding of the person to whom the staff member must report;
- a clearly written set of goals;
- a regular review of performance, both for the area of ministry and the staff person's performance in that ministry.

Sometimes pastors ask, "But how do I fire a volunteer?" The best answer that I've ever heard to that question was given by Marlene Wilson, one of the outstanding experts on volunteerism in America. In a speech to a group of pastors in Denver, Colorado, in 1990, she outlined the following ways for pastors to deal with this. She suggested they: (1) provide a clear job description, listing expectations; (2) enforce accountability; (3) write down instances where a volunteer's performance is lacking; (4) meet with the volunteer to discuss problems; and (5) when all else fails, fire the person. She also noted that treating volunteers differently from paid staff negatively affects an organization's morale.

I should also mention two other inherent problems that come with staff. First, each staff member tends to develop a closer relationship than the pastor to the participants and leaders of their area of ministry. This means that problems or issues with or among staff are serious problems for the program church. One of the consistent skills the pastor must exercise is the ability to manage a harmonious and well-functioning staff. Along with this is the ability to hire, develop, and terminate staff.

When a pastor/staff member relationship goes badly, the termination of that staff member could cost the congregation a number of families, perhaps a whole subcongregation. What many pastors don't realize is that this is as true of the volunteer staff as it is of the paid staff.

Second, one must understand the key functions of staff. When a program church is healthy, the staff function is to raise up and empower lay leadership and ministry in their areas. Unfortunately, some staff members function as both the principal person leading and doing ministry. For example, a church could call a dynamic and charismatic youth pastor. For a while, such a person can gather together a substantial youth group. However, if this person does not involve other adult members of the congregation in a passion for youth ministry, when this person burns out or leaves the ministry could evaporate.

When I encounter a declining large congregation, I almost always see this pattern being acted out. The congregational leaders hire staff to carry out a ministry that the congregation once had a passion for doing. Unfortunately, no lay members today care passionately enough about this area to give time and leadership to it. Yet the congregation still expects this ministry to exist. It is fueled by nostalgia, not passion.

The Drift to Nostalgia

Under the able leadership of its outstanding choir director/organist, First United Methodist was known for its excellent music ministry. The organist developed a series of choirs to teach music to members. The congregation had, in addition to its 40-voice senior choir, a children's choir, a youth ensemble, a brass quartet, and two bell choirs.

In 1961, after a second change of pastors in three years, the music director took a new post in a large East Coast congregation. Ten years later, a third music director arrived, promising to

rebuild the music program and return it to the 1950s standard. First United Methodist had been the fastest-growing congregation in its rapidly expanding Midwest community and the music ministry was an important part of this. It was known most for its commitment to excellence.

Since she inherited a 20-voice volunteer choir, this new director quickly recruited students from the local liberal arts college to sing the lead in each of the four parts. She convinced the board and pastor to pay these students.

The music program improved dramatically, and the longer-tenured members were relieved to see the revitalization of worship. However, when their director retired 12 years later, the church had declined to an ASA of 260 people. Its budget had fallen in recent years and the new choir director arrived to find that funds for student leaders were no longer available.

The transformation from healthy, dynamic, lay ministry to an expensive, nostalgic congregation concerned with maintaining its way of worship had run its course. It is from such stories that the demise of large congregations are written.

3. The Multiple Matrix Congregation

Whereas staff and program are key characteristics of the program size church, they are essentially a byproduct of a more important issue. At the heart of the large congregation is a characteristic that makes being large and continuing to grow possible. A program size church is technically a "multiple matrix congregation." What does this mean?

Basically, it means that the church is made up of more than one congregation. The smaller family size and pastoral churches are essentially single-cell organisms; one congregation of people. However, the large church has learned the skill of being many congregations under one roof. In the small church, members are naturally expected to attend all the activities of the congregation. In the large church, members are expected to participate in the various areas of ministry that relate to their interests. This makes choice and options a high value of the larger church. Notice how well this fits the expectations of boomers and Gen-Xers.

Once at a leadership network conference, I heard Leith Anderson, senior pastor of Wooddale Community Church in Eden Prairie, Minnesota, tell a story that demonstrates the dynamics of the larger church. Pastor Anderson had arrived back in his hometown airport of Minneapolis from a speaking engagement, but needed to make a correction in another ticket. He found himself speaking to a young woman at the airline's ticket counter. At the end of the conversation, she looked up at Pastor Anderson and said, "Mr. Anderson, will you be staying in town for the weekend?" When he said yes, she added, "Then please consider joining our church for worship." Needless to say, Leith was impressed by the young woman's eagerness to invite a total stranger. Then he asked what church she belonged to. He was startled to have her reply, "Wooddale Community Church!"

Obviously, he didn't recognize her, but more important, she didn't recognize the senior pastor of her congregation. Why? As he talked with her, he found out that she had been active in the young-professional group and attended the Saturday evening service. Although he had preached at that service regularly, she had never sat close enough to recognize him outside of worship.

Now if you are a pastor and are very uncomfortable with this story, you will want to serve a smaller congregation. In a large church, people often connect much better with an area of ministry and a staff member than with the senior pastor.

In the actual structure of the large church, a multiple matrix congregation is a series of overlapping circles of fellowship, service, study, or relationship that makes up a subcongregation of this larger unit. Large congregations have an amazing ability to launch these kinds of ministry, and they expect them to be well organized and done with excellence!

4. A Congregation of Excellence

This brings us to one other area that distinguishes the large church from smaller ones. The large program sized congregation uses a word seldom if ever used in smaller congregations: *Excellence!*

If it's worth adding a new worship service to Saturday night, then the large church will not do it until it can be done with excellence. If the church needs a new contemporary music group to lead the Sunday night service, it won't introduce the group until it can perform with excellence. Why is this an important value?

Several years ago, I supplied services at a small Episcopal church in Cincinnati. This congregation was in sad shape. The 20 or so remaining members could not afford to heat the 500-seat worship building, so we did a simple service in the fellowship hall. We seldom sang hymns, but on Christmas we did. So on Christmas Eve, we held the service in the main church, fired up the furnace, and Agnes sat at the old organ and played. She only knew three carols. As I recessed out of the church for the end of the service, she began to play her only known Christmas postlude. I exited to "White Christmas." With our typical Episcopal snobbish attitude toward music, especially in liturgy, I had never heard anything like it in an Episcopal church. But it didn't matter for several reasons.

First, we had no visitors that evening. Second, no one else could play a keyboard instrument. Third, and most important, we all loved Agnes. She did the best she could on that evening. I will never forget the experience. You see, small churches are about relationships, not about excellence.

The large church never behaves this way. There are two essential reasons for this. First, the congregation is too large to allow relationships to trump quality. Second, the large church is keenly aware that as much as 20 percent of any congregation are guests and not members of the congregation. The large church, therefore, has a natural sensitivity to the newcomer, the visitor, and the seeker that demands excellence as a standard.

Several years ago, Saint John the Divine Episcopal Church, in Houston, decided to offer a second major service at 11 A.M. on Sunday. Their reason was simple. They were out of space even with six weekend services. Since the senior pastor, Larry Hall, still cared about growth and evangelism, he decided that the church needed another option. Here is what they created:

- Parallel to their main 11 A.M. service held in their 500-seat worship center, they started in their family-life center a "contemporary worship service."
- Since the 11 A.M. service in the main building was somewhat formal, the parallel service was advertised as being casual. "Come in your jogging clothes if you like."
- Whereas the service was built around Communion (as is the custom in the Episcopal Church), Saint John's offered several creative alternatives in the worship. Most notable of these was the drama group that each week prepared a live skit to illustrate a reading from scripture.
- Because of the large church's desire for excellence, it went without saying that a superb music group was created to lead worship and that one of the key clergy would prepare an excellent sermon delivered in a free-flowing style.

Now all this is interesting, but what is more interesting is how the church prepared to offer this service. The senior pastor asked the staff to prepare and practice the service for one full year before it was advertised in the wider community. When I asked him why, he responded, "I wouldn't have been comfortable offering this service unless it was up to scale with the excellence of our other services." One year after the introduction of this service, the contemporary service had the same number of people as the formal 11 A.M. liturgy. Excellence was a key ingredient in accomplishing this, and is a key advantage of large congregations.

Yes, it is true that the small congregation can give you a chance to get to know Agnes. But it is also true that it is difficult to build a large church around the idiosyncrasies of one person.

In Summary

The program size church is very different from a pastoral size one. It is a staff-led, program-driven community with high standards in all activities of the congregation. It takes advantage of its size to build momentum. It uses need-based programs to create optional doorways into the congregation.

Most important for our observations, the large church is not a small church that has doubled in size. A large church is a different kind of community, a different system, and a different culture from a small church.

It is worth noticing how wide the gap is between the larger pastoral church of 150 and the beginning program church of 250. This explains why the transition from smaller to larger church is so difficult.

However, sometimes congregations fall in between these sizes. When they do, they have some particularly interesting dynamics. I call these congregations transitional size churches. They are the in-between congregations of America. Although they have great stress, they also have great potential. Let's turn our attention to these congregations.

Questions

1. What makes it possible for the large churches to have more than one congregation in them?

2. What is the relationship between the staff and the lay board in the operations of the larger church?

3. Why is it so hard to make excellence a standard for small churches?

4. If a program size church were in decline, at what level of attendance would the leadership begin to become anxious?

Chapter 7

Congregations in Transition

Obviously, between the pastoral size and program size congregations exists an area of transition. The pastoral size church functions well up to around 140 ASA. The program size church culture does not really get established till the church is over 225 ASA. This means that there is a large gap between the numbers of 140 to 225. Congregations in this gap are not part of a true culture. There is no system in this size that reinforces a congregational culture. They are simply too large to be a small church and too small to be a large church. However, they do share certain predictable characteristics.

Here then are four characteristics that transitional churches share in common.

- Transitional churches tend to be high-stress congregations for clergy. The expectations that the pastor's role will be primarily relational in the smaller church, and the expectations that accompany programs in the large church, create this high stress.
- Transitional churches tend to use up and burn out lay leaders. This size church has a shortage of real leaders. Therefore, the transitional size congregation tends to overuse its leaders and give them multiple jobs. This leads to high burnout.
- Transitional churches tend to need new programs, staff, and facilities *all at the same time*. This leads to confusion and a sense of continual frustration as the leaders run to keep up.

- Transitional congregations often experience tension and conflict as the congregation develops. Those who prefer the style of the smaller congregation often resent the changes. Those who want quality programs often find this resistance frustrating and irrational.

When a pastoral church grows past an ASA of 140, the pastor begins to lose the ability to maintain personal relationships with all members. However, the congregation does not have the ability to quickly shift to the larger program church approach. These congregations enter into a kind of limbo with certain predictable characteristics, the most important of which is the high stress on clergy and lay leadership. Transitional church leaders suffer high rates of burnout.

Again, it is important to remember that these churches do not represent a true church size and, therefore, they do not have a consistently reinforcing church culture. Consequently, their ASA can vary greatly each year along with the number of pledging units and other statistical information. Whereas a pastoral size congregation tends to report fairly consistent ASA over several years, not so for the transitional church. One year a transitional church can have an ASA of 185, but the next year it can be 167. This can be followed the next year with a figure of 192. These kinds of changes reflect the instability of this transition.

Occasionally, I do find a transitional church with a very consistent ASA. For example, I worked with a congregation whose ASA was consistently around 200. It did not take long to discover the reason for this. When I visited the church, I found a congregation that literally, every week, filled their inadequate worship space. This reflects a growing church inhibited simply by its lack of adequate space. These are the few congregations that you can assure, "Build it and they will come!" In these situations, the space is such an inhibition that a larger worship space will immediately allow for expansion.

Three Types of Transitional Churches

It is worth noting here that churches can get into the transitional size category in three different ways. Each of these ways has serious implications for the future development of these congregations.

The Overgrown Pastoral Church

Some transitional churches represent pastoral churches where the pastor has operated with high emotional energy and the ability to track relationships. These transitional churches are really overgrown pastoral churches that will probably adjust to a smaller size when there is a change of pastors.

The Hybrid Church

Second, some transitional churches represent pastoral churches that have discovered human-need ministries and activities that are the basic ingredients of an emerging program size church. These transitional churches represent underdeveloped program churches and are best served by reading the information in the next chapter and learning to act like a larger church.

The Declining Program Church

Third, some transitional churches were once larger congregations that, because of crisis, aging membership, or changing neighborhoods, have fallen below the program church size. These transitional churches are good candidates for revitalization, but they also operate with the remnant of past successful programs that no longer meet newcomer needs. Therefore, these churches need wise pruning and creative program development.

This third type of transition church illustrates a serious problem for larger churches that are in decline. Since the lower boundaries of a program church are around an ASA of 225, this means that it is difficult for leaders to grasp the serious nature of the decline and commit to addressing it with serious intention. For example, a once vibrant and active downtown parish with an ASA of 450 in the 1970s can slide slowly downward in size. Some leaders will be concerned, but if the congregation has resources such as capital or endowment funds, the slide is allowed to continue.

Sadly, once this church's ASA drops below the 225 level, the bells and whistles of alarm do go off, but the congregation has lost so much momentum that turning it around is difficult. Two dynamics further accentuate this difficulty. First, the community around the congregation has probably changed drastically so that present members are very unlike the present neighborhood. Second, once the alarms do go off, the maintenance of the facilities alone can take away all chance of capitalizing on any change in ministry direction. This is the story of the rusting hulks of former mainline churches that sit abandoned in many of our East Coast cities.

A Hybrid Church

The common transitional church has elements of both the pastoral and program churches present. This makes these congregations a kind of hybrid church. Leaders of these churches need to decide what kind of a congregation they should be. Unfortunately, leaders tend to have mixed expectations and communicate these expectations to present members and newcomers.

Most transitional congregations have high energy and communicate to newcomers that something special is happening in this community. However, the ambivalence about what size the church truly is often means that the incorporation tools are more related to the pastoral approach. This usually adds additional stress on the clergy as each new member comes expecting a claim to a relationship with the clergyperson. Abandoning the ways that have served the church well in the past is hard to do. However, for future effective growth, church leaders need to create a newcomer ministry that better reflects a program approach.

Some transitional congregations that were once larger do not communicate energy to new people. The half-empty building becomes a serious liability as newcomers wonder, "What happened?" These churches would do well to tell newcomers right up front what has happened and find ways to communicate that the church "is on the way back" and needs their help.

One such church that I worked with in inner-city Houston solved part of this problem by remodeling the worship space. The congregation took out several back pews. Then they added a space divider at the back and created a space for serving coffee and welcoming people as they entered the church. This, along with repainting a dreary and dark worship space, suddenly sent a new and more energetic message to member and newcomer alike.

Since few congregations decide that they would actually like to be smaller, it is best for leaders of transitional congregations to learn quickly how effective program churches operate and attract new people, then move in this direction. If a church remains in the transitional size too long, it tends to experience fatigue, and leadership burnout becomes a serious liability.

In Summary

The transition from a pastoral style church to a program size church is very difficult because the gap between these two churches is large and difficult to bridge. Oftentimes, transitional churches show a history of approaching program size levels several times and falling back. This falling back is the result of two issues that transitional church leaders must face. The first is lack of knowledge about how to act larger.

The second is that the transitional church often has long-term members who remember with nostalgia the good old days when they knew everyone in the church. These people often operate as a resistant group when their church attempts to create "new" ways of operating that resemble program size churches.

Let me add a last hopeful word about these churches. Because of the stress that already exists in the transitioning church, these congregations actually have great potential for growth. Once the leaders learn the skills necessary to make this transition to the program size, they have created a culture of growth that tends to continue for several years. It is not unusual to see growing transitional churches move quickly past long-established larger churches in size and energy. Now let's look at how this information on congregational sizes applies to pastors. I want to describe three pastors and how they dealt with growth.

Questions

1. What signs of stress do you see in your congregation?

2. What signs of conflicting expectations exist in your congregation?

3. What needs can you identify in program, staff, and facilities?

4. If your church is in the transitional size, which one of the three types of transitional churches are you?

Part Three

Types of Leaders

Chapter 8

Living with the Realities

My best friend, Robert Bethea, is a pastor. Rather, I should say that he *was* a great pastor. Recently, Parkinson's disease caused him to take early retirement. Often, during the summer, my wife and I would visit Bob and his wife, Judy. Of course, we attended church while there. The last time we visited, we experienced three things in the Sunday service that demonstrated his talent as a pastor.

First was the children's sermon. Early in the service, Bob invited all the younger children to come forward and join him for a story before they went to Sunday school. He sat down on the chancel steps with the children surrounding him. He reminded me of the storyteller doll of Navajo tradition. Bob had obviously prepared a story for the children related to the general theme of the day. However, Bob had a creative twist. He allowed the children to bring an object with them to the church. One or two of the children shared their objects—often a toy or household item—and Bob connected the objects with his story.

The kids loved this event and really connected to the challenge of the game—to stump their pastor. They often brought unusual objects. With an uncanny storyteller's ability, Bob would weave the objects into the story. The children sat attentively. They waited to see how Bob would connect the objects to the story. He always seemed able to make the connection between the objects and the central theme of the story. It was almost as if he already knew that morning what the objects would be. Needless to say, the adults sat attentive too.

Second, Bob was a storyteller-preacher. When he preached, he moved to the center aisle of the congregation.

While maintaining excellent eye contact, he proceeded to introduce his sermon with an engaging story or illustration. He preached like he was talking to each person individually. His sermons were take-home items. By this, I mean that they were applications of biblical truth to everyday life. His illustrations often came right out of his own experience.

The last sermon that I heard him preach was on suffering and unanswered prayer. He started with an illustration from a member of the parish struggling with cancer. I did not know the person, but obviously many did. His sermon was about 15 minutes long. Everyone connected. It was hopeful, personal, and engaging. It was not polished and his grammar and syntax were not always flowing. It didn't matter. He was their pastor!

Third, Bob added commentary to the set intercessions for the day. Even though the Episcopal Church has set prayers, Bob opened this segment of the service by giving a brief commentary on some current needs of congregational members. The community entered the prayers with serious concern for one another. His commentary enabled the community to both know and express mutual concerns.

After the service and lunch together, my wife and I returned home with Judy. Meanwhile, Bob went to the hospital. On the way home from the hospital he dropped by a leader's home to discuss a possible area of contention. They got it resolved.

When I asked Bob to tell me about his leaders, he never started with their skills or their present occupation. He started with their present issues and relationships. For example, if I asked him to tell me about his present stewardship leader, he might reply with something like this:

> Helen is a very caring person. She is probably too caring. Right now Helen and John [her husband] are taking care of their granddaughter while their daughter gets her life together. Their daughter went through a particularly difficult divorce last year.

Bob would forget to mention until the end that Helen is a very capable senior executive with a communications firm.

Bob was a great pastor. He could have been my pastor anytime. If I lived in his community, I would have attended his congregation. The church did not have a small-group ministry, it did not have much in the way of adult education, and it did not have lay visitation teams for visitors. It wouldn't matter to me much if it did. The church had Bob. He was their pastor. His emotional attention and caring connected to people and it also connected the people to one another. Let's take a closer look at Bob's story.

A Pastor's Story

Bob was a later vocation to the ministry. A former sales representative, Bob felt a call to the ministry in midlife. Although Bob was a successful salesman, he was surprised to discover how much he enjoyed the intellectual challenge of seminary. He was 42 when he was graduated and went to serve a congregation.

When Bob was graduated from seminary, he was assigned as an assistant to a midsized congregation with a female pastor. Bob got along well with the senior pastor, even though he often disagreed with her theological positions.

During his two years of working as an assistant, Bob made pastoral calls and assisted in the general ministries of the congregation. He was never given charge of a specific area, but would from time to time become involved in one. Two years into this assistantship, "he was ready for his first place."

Bob was called to restart a struggling mission congregation. This church, Saint Francis, was located in a fast-growing suburb of Seattle named Mill Creek. The church had never really gotten off the ground. When Bob arrived, there were between 25 and 30 people present at a regular Sunday service. The small congregation did not have a church building and worshiped in the fellowship hall. The parking lot wasn't paved, which was a real problem in

Seattle. The land on which the congregation met had serious environmental restrictions, which meant that adding to the buildings was always a hassle. I first met Bob three years after he had become the pastor of Saint Francis.

During his time there, the congregation had grown. They were now over 100 ASA. They were overcrowding every inch of space. In the time he was pastor, the congregation remodeled their worship space twice, added two new classroom buildings, created a lay visitation ministry to the elderly and homebound, and created an innovative Christian education program for children. Every year, Bob presented a dozen folks to be confirmed, and performed several adult baptisms, usually of formerly nonchurched men.

Seeking Growth Advice

After we became friends, Bob learned that I had some expertise in congregational development. He would regularly ask me for advice. He knew that Saint Francis had tremendous growth potential based on the growth of the area. He was pleased as he shepherded the congregation to more than 150 attendees each Sunday. Then things began to slow down.

One day over coffee, he sought my advice on a particular matter. "I've designed a new committee system for our lay board," he volunteered. "Let me show you this diagram." I looked at a flowchart that showed his board branching off into nine committees. "I am going to ask each of my nine board members to function as a liaison to each of these areas. Then at each board meeting, instead of having to micromanage each area, we will just hear a report. After all," he added, "our present meetings go on for three to four hours and we end up tired and stressed out! This is not good for my leadership's morale." I nodded in agreement to this last statement.

After some time, he asked, "What do you think?"

"What do I think about what?" I replied.

"What do you think about the chart?" he added with exasperation.

I pondered it for several minutes. Finally, I gave him the answer that has now become a standard for me in dealing with the pastors of transitional sized congregations, "This is one of the best flowcharts that I've ever seen."

He smiled for a few minutes and then began to ponder what I had actually said. "Wait a minute," he stammered, "something's wrong with what you just said."

"I said it was a great chart, what more do you want me to say?" I gave him a slight grin.

"I want to know if it will work!" he added with energy.

"Bob, let me ask you a question," I replied. "Which of these committees, if you could only have one, do you really need *right now*?"

"That's easy," he quickly replied. "The Newcomer Committee. I need some help in keeping track of all the visitors and newcomers."

"Then create that committee, get a good person to lead it—forget the board member idea—and help get the committee up and running," I advised.

"OK," he responded. "Now tell me why."

"Think about your business experience," I cautioned. "What company, in its right mind, would add nine new divisions at the same time?" I could see the dawn of recognition on his face.

Under his direction, Saint Francis reached an ASA of 185. He continued to ask me for advice and I continued to offer it. Coincidentally, during this time, Judy took a job as "newcomer minister" for a large and growing Methodist church. When I offered advice, she would often comment, "See, Bob, didn't I tell you?" He would shrug off her comment with something like, "Yes, but we weren't ready for that when you suggested it."

A New Call

After twelve years in Mill Creek, Bob was called to be pastor of another Seattle congregation, Resurrection, in

Bellevue. This congregation had once been much larger, but was now down to 60 people. They had a large church building that doubled as parish hall and worship space, and had built a retirement community on the back of their property. They had once had an average attendance of around 220 people. Then the pastor left and his tenure was followed by four years of constant conflict with the new pastor. When that pastor was finally forced to leave, they were down to the 60 worshipers. They jumped at the opportunity to have Bob become their pastor.

At first he was reluctant to leave Saint Francis, but the constant wear of inadequate space, land issues, and low salary forced him to consider the change. Four years later, the new congregation was back to 110 to 120 a Sunday.

On my last visit with him, he asked me, "What do I need to do to help this congregation break the 200 Barrier?"

This time I was prepared for him. I told him, "Bob, you are my best friend, so listen to me. Don't worry about breaking the 200 Barrier. You were called here to rebuild this congregation and you are doing a terrific job! Attendance is back up, stewardship is the best that it has ever been, and people are feeling hopeful and optimistic. You are a great pastor and they love you. You could be my pastor anytime. I suspect that this congregation will continue to grow over the next few years. When you retire, however, the best thing you could do for them is leave them feeling good about themselves. Constantly worrying about breaking the 200 Barrier will only make them anxious and then they will perform badly. Just love them, keep sharp, spend more time with Judy, and play a little more golf."

My Advice

If you have read the other chapters, you already understand my advice. I wanted to communicate several things to my friend. Among these are the following:

- You have learned to be a very effective pastor of a community numbering between 60 and 80 families.
- You have a demonstrated track record of development and growth with congregations of this size.
- You came to the right place, they needed you, and you are blessing them.
- You are a successful revitalization pastor for this present congregation.
- If you attend to your own mental and physical health, give priority to your wife, and just relax and don't overwork, your natural skills will shine.
- I love and need you as a friend, so don't work yourself to death.
- Health, not growth, should be the pastor's goal in the setting you now have.

And finally, I acknowledged to myself that changing the behavior patterns of a 60-year-old man is nearly impossible! These behaviors had served him well, so why change them anyway?

All across America, there are pastors like Bob in all denominations. They are terrific pastors. In many seminars and books, they are being told that growing the church beyond the pastoral size is important and that they should learn how to do this. They are adding to the already existing stress of the emotional care of their people a false and, at times, demonic expectation that they should be something they are not.

Sometimes when people in my denomination introduce me at meetings as a church growth officer, I always correct them with, "I am the Congregational Development Officer." Sometimes as congregations develop, they grow. Whereas some congregations have growth potential, all have developmental issues. My friend Bob was not only a good pastor; he had developed and grown both the congregations that he served.

Living with the Realities

Could my friend Bob serve a larger congregation? Absolutely! If he were called to a congregation with 300 people attending each Sunday, he would do just fine. He would probably both develop and grow it. Was Bob the kind of transformational leader who can lead a congregation from the pastoral to the program size? Probably not. But the point of Bob's story is that growth is seldom the measurement of pastoral effectiveness.

If you are the pastor of a congregation with fewer than 150 people attending each Sunday, learn how to pastor effectively and do not measure yourself and your effectiveness by growth alone. It may be the American way—or at least the Southern California way—to measure your effectiveness by growth, but it is seldom God's way and it is almost never your people's way.

Now let's look at a pastor who led a church from small size to large.

Questions

1. What skills made Bob such an effective pastor for the churches he served?

2. What do you think of my advice to Bob?

3. What would you have advised him to do?

Chapter 9

Living with the Transition

When John Wengrovius became the pastor of Calvary Church in Golden, Colorado, he was faced with a dilemma that many pastors face in America. He inherited a small, historic, downtown congregation that wanted to grow. However, even though the leadership wanted the congregation to grow, Calvary faced enormous challenges to this task.

The church building sat on the side of a hill in the center of Golden. It had been built when the town was much smaller. Over the years, Golden had grown to be a premier suburb of the Denver area, situated at the base of the Rocky Mountains. The congregation had learned over the years to fit its buildings. The main church was actually a quaint little chapel. It would seat comfortably 80 people. Adjacent to it was a small parish hall and kitchen facility. There was no classroom space. The church had no off-street parking, although they did have use on Sunday of the town parking lot opposite the church site. This meant that midweek, they had no dedicated parking at all.

When John arrived, he found a pastoral size congregation averaging around 140 people each Sunday morning. This congregation fit the church by having two services. The first was a traditional 8 A.M. service. Such services are often made up of older-generation people, many of whom are retired. They also had a more family-oriented 10 A.M. service. John and his young family fit the profile of those who attended this later service.

John is a very loving, thoughtful pastor with a strong

commitment to good liturgy, effective pastoral care, and dedicated Christian education for all ages. His winsome personality, combined with his native Colorado outlook, made him a great pastor for this church. He took the position at Calvary knowing that the growing community meant that the church had tremendous potential.

As he predicted, this pastoral church continued to grow. However, given the serious limitations of the buildings, growth for Calvary was problematic from the beginning. Over his first five years, John also introduced several innovations for a pastoral size church. He added to the traditional choir program a more contemporary music group. He added several tiers to the adult education program. He was able to recruit a deacon for his church whose specialty was community service. She was extremely successful in building a bridge between Calvary and various social agencies in the Golden area.

All this brought to this historic pastoral church some programmatic elements. The result was steady growth for Calvary. Early on, the church made adjustments to this growth by adding additional Sunday services and a Saturday evening service. In order to accommodate more people at the main Sunday service, the leaders removed the windows between the church and the parish hall. Since the two building were attached, this opened up additional space for seating. Unfortunately, it also compromised the only space for Christian education.

One solution to all these problems was considered in the early days of John's tenure. Why not simply sell the present building and relocate to more ample space outside of the downtown area? The leaders of Calvary actively considered this idea. However, over the years, all the other denominational churches in the downtown area had relocated. The leadership of Calvary felt strongly that Calvary should continue its witness and presence in the downtown area. They made the critical decision not to relocate.

When I first encountered Calvary Church, the congregation was very active and highly stressed. The congregation was continuing to grow, but the space limitations created constant problems. There was a sense of excitement but also a sense of urgency. Every solution seemed to create more problems, and this added to the stress of the leaders.

Some of the issues were not so apparent to the general membership. Because there were a number of weekend services, most of the membership experienced Calvary as a very small and intimate congregation. Many liked this feeling. Few, other than the leaders and staff, really understood how large the congregation had actually become.

The staff had begun to grow. These were hard-working and dedicated people, most of whom were members of the church. Some of them also loved the small quaintness of the church and their easy access to the rector. In the early days of the growth, the addition of each new staff member meant a new supervisory relationship for John. This added to his responsibilities.

John was committed to growth and reaching new families. His easy and relaxed personality and pastoral style meant that he was frequently in demand. He was expected to attend all activities in the congregation. Much of the congregation's life centered around John's ministry. His calendar and the church's calendar were essentially the same thing. As the church grew, so did the number of relationships he had to maintain. As it grew, John had more and more events to attend. In short, he was exhausted and overworked. He asked for my help.

Beginning the Transition

My first work was with the staff. We spent a day looking at the organization of the growing congregation. On a large white board we listed every organization and ministry and drew lines of accountability and responsibility. After several hours, we had created a dramatic rendition of crossover lines and complexity. At the center of everything was the pastor.

Over the years, I have repeated this exercise with numerous transitional size congregations. I continue to be amazed at the complicated social structure that exists in such congregations. I am also amazed at how all these lines lead eventually to the pastor.

The staff was caught up in the energy of the exercise and had become engaged with the diagram. John, however, had begun to get quieter and quieter. Finally, I asked him, "John, what's wrong?"

He responded, "No wonder I am so worn out and exhausted. I get tired just looking at all this." He went on to describe how complex all of these relationships were. "How can I continue to work under these conditions?" he asked. Of course, he could not. Then we began a long process of reorganizing the congregation.

Many years ago, a top-level executive taught me about "span of control." This refers to the actual number of people or things that one person can direct. He pointed out that many executives greatly overestimate their ability to manage a large number of events, people, or things. He shared with me a very valuable principle that I shared with John and his staff and continue to share today. A person's span of control is no more than two digits! In other words, if a pastor is directly responsible for managing more than nine areas at once, the areas begin to manage the pastor.

I have worked with pastors who had as many as 28 people and areas to manage. They have the illusion that they are managing these areas. In truth, the squeaky wheel and the immediate crisis drive the system. We set out to create a system with John having only seven areas of responsibility. We limited this to seven because this was a growing congregation and it needed to free John up to create new areas of ministry and allow for future staff.

At times, the staff members were resistant to changes. I found the resistance centered around two things. First, the staff resisted having direct lines of accountability, which made for a situation where it was hard to hold individuals responsible for what did not work. Second, the staff liked John and wanted to maintain casual and close relationships with him. This was most often expressed when staff dropped by the pastor's office and said, "Pastor, got a minute?" An hour or so later, they left. When this happened, it was often unclear whether they worked for the pastor or whether the pastor worked for them.

As John shared this information with church leaders, the need for changes became clearer. This created another set of issues at times. Despite all the discussion about change, it was often slow to develop. Staff and leaders would become discouraged or frustrated when they could not see immediate results. They became tired and a bit cynical about the need for change.

With coaching and the support of a few key lay leaders, John began to make some changes in the way he operated as the leader of the congregation. One of the first decisions was to change the way the staff related to him. Of course, it was easier to do this when new staff were hired, rather than changing current staff member's habits. Over time, some things got better. The church continued to grow, yet the stress on John continued.

Then John and his leadership began to make some changes in how they made decisions and delegated responsibilities. Again, there was resistance to these changes. Some board members liked the hands-on management that they had experienced in the smaller Calvary. Eventually, most of these people rotated off the board.

Finally, the leaders began to develop a long-range plan for the development of Calvary. They put together a comprehensive plan for the expansion of the church. Early on, the leadership met with a consultant who pointed out two important issues.

First, he pointed out that the worship center was the key to growth. They needed to address this facility issue first. Second, he recommended that they take the time and spend the money to develop a full site plan for the future Calvary.

This would prevent short-term solutions from interfering with long-term development. These two pieces of advice proved invaluable in the days ahead.

Because much of this plan involved creating more space, it meant Calvary would have to purchase expensive downtown property and build new facilities. I should also mention that because of environmental restrictions and other legal issues, this plan took several years to implement. This created a delay between starting capital campaigns and being able to see the tangible results of such giving.

The congregation was generally supportive of the plan and gave generously toward the first of what became five capital fund campaigns. In the second campaign to build a new worship center, John and the leadership hit on a creative idea. One Sunday, they moved all services to a local high school for "One Great Time of Worship Together!" It was the first time that most of the congregational members saw how large the church had become. They were pushing toward a 200 average Sunday attendance.

One important payoff of staying downtown is that Calvary has been able to acquire a number of large grants from other nonprofit organizations to accomplish this work. Most of these grants came from members' relationships to other organizations. Without these grants, this work might not have happened.

Paying the Price

Calvary now has a larger worship space. The town of Golden has even given them permission to close a side street and connect to another piece of property for further expansion. The congregation lived through 12 years of being a transitional size congregation. Average attendance has now risen to more than 225 and continues to grow.

The congregation has paid a high price for this transition. Financially, the church has had to raise a considerable sum of money and incur a large amount of debt. Much of the capital improvements was foundational and involved land. Often it took quite a while to see the results of a campaign. This delay has slowed growth because some members simply did not want to pay this price or became discouraged. Some key lay leaders burned out through all this.

It goes without saying that John paid a high price in all this too! He had frequently questioned how much longer he could live through this transition and stress. He has been constantly stretched as a pastor. He has had conflicting expectations projected upon him by various church members. The question we may want to ask is, how long can a pastor live through such transition?

I believe that John is exceptional. I generally advise pastors not to stay more than five years in a transitional size congregation. Primarily, I advise this for two reasons:

- Chronic stress is dangerous to a person's health. The stress that a pastor feels amid the conflicting expectations, both internal and external, can disable even the most dedicated and committed pastor.
- Stress can also lead a pastor to act out in inappropriate ways. Under chronic stress, pastors can abuse alcohol or other drugs, act out sexually, or lose perspective and make bad decisions in the management of money.

John has been able to live with this stress for a very long time. Here are some of the ways he does it.

- As an introvert, he has a strong inner spirituality that allows him to reflect and think through his situation.
- He loves the Golden area and wants to serve there.
- He stays connected to the wider church.
- He remains a lifelong learner, attending conferences and gaining new insights as a leader.
- He has extraordinary lay leadership who support him through these changes.

- He attends to tension and conflict in effective ways when they occur in the congregation.
- He has a tenacious and persistent personality that has allowed him to stick with the challenge and see it through.

When I asked what John would add to this list, he responded:

- a loving and supportive wife;
- having an effective mentor;
- strong peer support from a few key clergy friends.

Do I recommend that pastors follow John's example? No, I do not. But, I do think that some small congregations can go through such a transition and overcome seemingly overwhelming odds when they have dedicated pastors who persist through the obstacles and supportive lay leadership that continues to work and sacrifice toward the greater vision.

Questions

1. What were John's resources in leading through this long transition?

2. What lesson can other small congregations learn from Calvary?

Chapter Ten

Leading through the Transition

When Ted Nelson came out of seminary, the bishop of the Episcopal Diocese of Dallas assigned him to a struggling new mission in a growing Dallas suburb. Ted entered seminary after a successful career as a regional sales manager for a food company. He arrived at his new job energetic and enthusiastic only to find the small mission mired in interpersonal problems and lacking commitment to growth. After initially sorting out the leadership, Ted was left with a small group of about 60 regular worshipers.

Ted has a heart for helping people. Soon he was not only leading this growing church but he was also working on a degree in marriage and family counseling. In addition to the regular pastoral load of the congregation, his pursuit of this degree meant that he was regularly assigned clients to counsel.

Soon Ted was engaged in 50-hour workweeks, and his usual energetic personality began to show wear and tear. He found himself exhausted a great deal of the time. He felt this was somewhat justified by the escalating growth of his congregation to nearly 150 worshipers per Sunday. As the number of parishioners increased, so did the pastoral demands on his time. He began to wonder how long he would be able to keep up this demanding emotional pace.

One day a member of the congregation approached him with a pastoral issue. Her son was serving time in the Huntsville State Prison. She poured out her mother's concern for this misunderstood child who just needed someone to care for him. She believed that if Ted could just go and visit her son, it would make all the difference in the world.

She hoped that having such a loving pastor connect with her son would help turn his life around! Like the persistent widow of the scriptures, she continued to pressure Ted to make a visit.

Ted knew that the chance of such a visit affecting this young man was very small. He had been around enough to know that the woman was just grasping at straws. He wanted to help her, but he also knew that the four-hour drive to Huntsville from Dallas for a 15-minute visit was poor use of his time and emotional energy. Then, in addition, he would have the four-hour return drive. When would he get time for this?

While all this was happening, Ted's wife Lee Ann began to complain about how little time they had for each other. Ted seldom ever took his day off. He was often out in the evenings at church meetings or doing counseling. Like many transitional church pastors, Ted was feeling the effects of the increasing demands on his life.

One day he surprised his wife when he announced that they should take his day off and drive out into the country for a picnic. He explained that this way they would be able to get away from the demands of the church and spend some time together. Lee Ann thought this was a great idea, but she was a little cautious. She asked him where he would like to go and was surprised when he suggested Huntsville. She pointed out that this was a very long trip, no little drive into the country, and asked why he wanted to go there. He pointed out that this way he could visit his member's incarcerated son.

The cat was out of the bag. Lee Ann knew perfectly well that Ted was stumbling around trying to meet both personal needs and the unrealistic demands of congregational members. Still she agreed. She decided to take whatever time with him she could get.

On the way to Huntsville, Ted and Lee Ann began to talk about their lives and the demands of this successful and growing congregation. Ted poured out his feelings of frustration and tiredness. He also shared the hopelessness he had begun to feel. It seemed the more he worked, the more work there was for him to do. It wasn't that it was unproductive work; he could see the fruit of much of his labor. He felt that the success created its own demands. They were able to do little that morning except share their mutual concerns. Finally, Ted suggested that they change the subject and he asked Lee Ann to read the appointed scripture passage for morning prayers that day.

Lee Ann began to read from Exodus 18. It was the story of Moses and Jethro. Moses was exhausting himself leading the people of Israel when his father-in-law Jethro paid him a visit. It's easy to imagine that part of this story is based on the complaints of Jethro's daughter about the demands on Moses' family life.

"What you are doing is not good!" offers Jethro to the overworked Moses. He points out that Moses sits each day judging the people of Israel one at a time and they stand in line waiting for him. Jethro tells Moses that he is wearing out both himself and his people. "What else can I do?" asks the worn-out Moses.

Jethro suggests that Moses appoint elders to judge the people. They can do the regular work and bring Moses the hard cases. Moses thinks this advice is good and godly. He appoints elders and the situation improves. This whole incident may be the first biblical example of a management consultant.

Suddenly Ted swerved the car to the side of the road. Excitedly, he interrupted Lee Ann. He pointed out how God was speaking to them about his stress and overcommitment. Ted saw how God was speaking to them about the church. He believed he had heard God's answer. He just needed to find people to help him pastor the congregation. They could do the regular work and refer the difficult cases to him!

Ted chose to make this work by forming small home-fellowships. He abandoned a great deal of the church's regular programs and began to identify and train 35 couples to pastor people by leading these groups. He gave himself to this work as energetically as he had in pastoring the whole congregation. He set a goal to get 100 percent of his people into these small groups.

Within two years, the congregation had taken off. The number of small groups began to grow. Ted and his leaders developed an effective incorporation ministry that quickly tied new people to newly forming small groups. The training of group leaders continued. Although the church was unable to get 100 percent of its members into small groups, it did get a very high percentage involved. Over the next few years, Ted grew one of the largest Episcopal congregations in the country. Over the next 15 years, the church went through four building drives, built a Christian counseling center, and sent scores of missionaries into Christian service.

The Leader's Blind Spot

Ted illustrates a truth about transforming pastoral churches into larger ones. When this happens, it usually comes about not as a result of a new program; it is usually the result of a transformed leader. Transformational leaders are able to grow, change, and adapt their style to meet the needs of the community. Ted did not go from being a "shepherd" to a "rancher" as some church-growth experts would suggest. He always remained, at heart, a pastor. Ted grew the church by deciding to work *through* others rather than work directly *with* others. He did, however, work *through* them using his primary skills. He did not become a manager; he remained a shepherd. He gave himself as a leader to the few to benefit the many. It is important to remember that the few didn't need him; he needed them.

Professor Charles Gangel in his book *Feeding and Leading* reflects on the event in the life of Moses that spoke to Ted. He points out that Moses could not figure out the solution by himself. It wasn't that he was dumb or not skilled as a leader. Gangel points out that the first impulse of a true leader is to stand up to the task. It is precisely those qualities that made Moses a leader that blinded him to the next step as a leader. Things haven't changed much from the days of Moses. Most successful leaders continue to redo, replay, and use the skills that they know will work, until, for some reason, they no longer work. Then, by the grace of God, if a Jethro comes along, or an unhappy spouse, there comes a possible moment of insight. Sometimes this insight is followed by a determined decision to persist in a new way of behaving. When this happens, transformation is possible.

Several years ago, after reading church-growth books on the programs and ministries that help break the 200 Barrier, I decided to check out their assumptions. They hadn't worked for me and I wondered why. I identified several pastors who had broken the so-called 200 Barrier and I went and interviewed them. Not one of them told me a story about a program. They all, like Ted, told me a life transformation story.

Such leaders are hard to find. Most of us just keep replaying our skills and successes. When things don't go well, we work harder. When we finally collapse, we feel as though we failed. Some leaders find a more excellent way. They become "transformational leaders."

If I could package transformational leadership, I would make a fortune as a consultant. In the twelfth chapter, we will take a look at the characteristics of a transformational leader. For now, we will turn to the issue of applying this information to learn what a church needs to do to transform from a small congregation into a large one.

Questions

1. What were the key elements in Pastor Ted's personal transformation?

2. Why is delegating tasks such a hard thing to do?

3. What traditional roles of pastor could be delegated to other members of the congregation?

4. What is the difference between "programs" and "transformation"?

Chapter 11

Resistance

In the stories of the three pastors we have read about in this section, we have been looking at how their leadership styles dealt with the realities of transforming from a small to a large church. In each of these examples we can see the resistance factors that tend to pull the congregation back down to a smaller size. In this chapter, we will take a closer look at this resistance.

A few years ago, I was leading a seminar for pastoral size congregations. During this seminar, I spent some time talking about the difficulties of growing a pastoral size congregation into a larger programmatic one. This led to a typical interaction with congregational leaders of pastoral size congregations concerning their congregations' resistance to change.

Under one section on why the small church remains small, I presented three basic organizing principles of a pastoral size church. (Note these were Episcopal congregations, so the third one particularly fits them.)

- *The church is organized around the village.* In the village, everyone knows one another. We follow Paul's admonition, "Rejoice with those who rejoice; mourn with those who mourn" (Rom. 12:15 NIV). Since the congregation is less than 150 worshipers, it is possible for all members to be aware of the needs of others in this community. (Remember the Rule of 150!)
- *The church is organized around the pastor.* Since an ordinary person would be able to track between

60 to 80 households without losing track of some of the sheep, the congregation is limited in size. To exceed this number would put stress on the pastor.

- ***The church is organized around the church year.*** The leaders are focused on having Lent again. They will plan out the Christmas season based on what was done last year. Once more, they will organize a church school for the fall. The leaders are, therefore, focused on repeating each event. They may wish to make incremental improvements, but not make substantial changes.

I went on to suggest that these dynamics interacting with one another make for a powerful resistance force toward substantial growth. Since the people in the room seemed to be nodding their heads in agreement, I asked, "What else could you organize the church around?"

Now, I have asked this question of literally hundreds of leaders—lay and clergy—of pastoral size churches. In each setting, I have seldom received any response. The same happened that day. The leaders are so accustomed to the system that they cannot imagine any other way. It is beyond their imagination and off their radar screen. I usually just move on with my presentation.

Occasionally, one participant might interject a question at this point, such as, "What else could you organize around?" Drawing on my experience with a wide variety of larger churches, I offer a sample list:

- Ministering to children both inside and outside the congregation
- Making disciples
- Reaching seekers
- Touching the unchurched
- Forming Christians through small groups
- Reaching out to the poor and needy

I then add, "Some churches organize singularly around one of these." I then push them to look at how a church organized around "reaching seekers" would have a different organizing set of ministries and strategies. At this point, the leaders of small churches are now on transformational ground. A typical response is, "Why would you want to organize church in this way? It wouldn't look like church." Of course, it would not look like a small church.

In this particular seminar, one leader seemed distressed and wanted to explore this further with me. He challenged me by saying, "Suppose we agree as a church that we want to substantially grow our congregation and do the great commission. You make it sound impossible. Could you tell us how to do both?"

This is the kind of interaction that a consultant and seminar leader often wants to have. So I offered this challenge: "I will tell you how to do it, but at the end I am going to ask you two challenging questions, so please take notes." I then gave the group the example of Pastor Sally.

Pastor Sally and Dramatic Change

There was once a small congregation that decided it needed to change. The church had never seemed to get off the ground. Its attendance had never exceeded 100. Every time things seemed to be going well, something would happen. Often that something was a change in pastors.

After its last change in pastors, the attendance had dropped back to 80 people. The leaders were so discouraged that they decided to take a radical step. They went to their judicatory leaders and asked for help. They explained that they really wanted to carry out the great commission. They begged to be given a pastoral leader who could help them reach the unchurched and grow. After being convinced of their desire to make serious changes, the denomination sent them Sally.

Sally was not a typical pastor. First, she was a female

pastor in a congregation that had never before had a female pastor. Second, she was not trained in one of their denomination's seminaries. Third, she had been a very successful businesswoman who had started her own business before her call to ministry. All these factors offered challenges, but the congregation and its leaders were serious about making the change. Over the next two years, Sally led the congregation through significant change and substantial growth.

First, she abandoned all organizations in the congregation. Then, she organized a Saturday planning day and invited all the members so that she could identify what the members really thought was important. Two areas emerged: mutual support in growth as Christians, and concern about the children in the church and the community.

In response to these two concerns, she listed each of these areas on large sheets of paper:

- Small groups
- Church school
- Outreach ministry to children

She then asked each member to sign on to one area where he or she would be willing to work for the next two years. People could only sign up with one of these areas.

Sally explained that this list now represented the organization and ministries of this congregation. The congregation would meet each Sunday for worship, but each of the three groups would start meeting individually to find ways in which to carry out ministry in each of these areas.

Sally began the small-group area by selecting small-group coordinators. Over the next few months, she trained them how to run a home group. She helped them understand that small groups have been proved to be the best methodology for both mutual support and discipleship formation. Once the congregation agreed to the small-group plan, she established that each group would invite nonchurch members to participate in each of the three groups. Finally, when each group reached 12 members, the groups divided into two groups of six each and continued to invite others to join.

The church school ministry organized in a fairly predictable manner with teachers and students. Since there were not enough students to fill a class for each grade, Sally suggested that the children invite their friends to fill a class. Soon the intergenerational church school was growing.

The third area of ministry focused on two critical needs of children in the community. Since the church was surrounded by working-class families, often with both parents working, the church decided to offer an after-school program that provided tutoring and meals for children. The church quickly got a grant from a local organization to provide computers for the classrooms, and the work of developing and growing the congregation began.

Sally aimed her work on Sunday around two themes for the next two years. First was a basic set of interesting sermons on the person and work of Jesus of Nazareth. Since this sermon series did not exactly fit her denomination's three-year lectionary, she ignored the lectionary. Second, she organized worship with a goal of reaching a "target" audience of 35-year-old nonchurch couples with small children.

In two years, the church grew quickly. Since the small church building would not hold everyone, the service was moved to a local school until a larger facility could be built. At the end of the second year, the church had grown from 80 in attendance to more than 300.

Can This Work?

After telling the group about Pastor Sally's congregation, I then asked the people in the room, "Could this work for you?" After an animated and excited conversation, they agreed that it could. I shared with them that it had worked for many church leaders. It works frequently in new congregations. Sally was actually a composite of a few church planters that I had known.

The Myth *of the* 200 Barrier

I then asked them to list the major transitions the church would have to go through to make all this work. They made a dynamic list that nailed all the critical points of change. Among these were:

- Reorganizing the church around passion and needs
- Streamlining the structure
- Being entrepreneurial toward the unchurched
- Making children and parents the focus of much the congregation did
- Using small groups to build closeness and build up Christians

Again, I asked them, "So, do you think this would work?" They enthusiastically agreed. Then I asked, "So, why won't you now go and do this?" There was a very long silence in the room. Finally, a wise, gray-haired woman raised her hand and I called on her. Slowly she stood up, looked around, and then said, "I can tell you why we won't do this. It comes down to two simple truths. First, where are we going to find our Sally? Second, you started with 'She abandoned all organizations in the congregation.' No church represented in this room would agree to this as a starting point."

Of course, she was absolutely right. Her first observation focused on the difficult issue of finding a transformational leader. Most denominational systems acculturate their clergy to their system. Many denominational systems involve a committee of present pastors and lay leaders who screen the candidates for ordained ministry. This process of selection and acculturation is intended to select people who will be happy running the present models of ministry, not find people capable of transforming a system. Where indeed would they find their Sally?

Her second observation focused on the issue of organizational resistance. She correctly noticed that Sally began her process by abandoning the present system. This would have included the present elected lay governance board. Can you imagine how difficult this would be in an existing congregation? What right would a pastor have to discontinue the duly elected and legally standing body? You might ask why Sally needed to do this. Could she merely have abandoned all the other structures? This question leads us to a very important point about leaders in small churches.

Rabbi Ed Friedman once suggested that what you see in nature, you often see reproduced in the human community. He pointed out that in nature about 10 percent of an organism's cells self-differentiate toward "headship" functions. He noted that when a group of people takes on a task, about 10 percent of them function in some sort of leadership capacity. Further, in most congregations, leaders comprise about 10 percent of the average worship attendance.

If you follow his reasoning (and I have found it to be very true) this means that most congregations greatly overestimate the actual numbers of real leaders they have. A congregation with only 80 people can easily have 15 to 20 leadership roles. This leads to two of the most common problems of small congregations.

When you have fewer leaders than you have leadership roles, the congregation usually has only two alternatives: allow present leaders to occupy more than one leadership role, or allow nonleaders to occupy leadership roles.

The problem with solution number one is that this makes the congregation very vulnerable to the emotional well-being and family health of the person occupying these roles. The congregation will directly feel any dysfunction in this person or this person's family.

The problem with solution number two is subtler, but in the long run it is more pervasive. When you mix nonleaders with leaders, the nonleaders have a restraining effect upon the real leaders who are present.

What Sally knew was that in starting up three new areas for ministry, she had a leadership problem. She simply did not have enough leaders. In addition, the leaders she predictably had were already on a committee whose primary purpose was maintaining the existing structure. By abolishing this group, she was able to allow leaders to assign themselves to areas of ministry according to their own interests and passion.

Finally, we can note that the church planter does not have an already existing structure and is free to organize around felt needs and ministry opportunities.

Summary

Many smaller congregations could find a dramatic new ministry and life if they were willing to start with this basic challenge: abandon the present way of organizing and organize around felt need and passion. Of course, this would be resisted strongly in any existing organization. This resistance would be presented in all kinds of justifying language. Among these we might list:

- The bylaws would never permit this.
- This is contradictory to our denomination's way of doing things.
- You are giving the pastor too much power.
- You are taking power away from the lay board.
- You are risking the complete breakdown of the congregation.
- You will make the present members angry.
- You will upset the present leadership.
- Who will be responsible for paying the bills or mowing the grass?

At the heart of all these lies the core of resistance. What is this resistance? We have seen it already. It is: the status quo; the way things are around here; the congregational culture.

Questions

1. Why does organizing around felt need and ministry opportunity allow a congregation to grow, whereas organizing around denominational requirements does not allow similar growth?

2. How could you bring about such a radical reorganizing in an existing congregation?

3. What percentage of existing small congregations would be willing to undertake such radical revision of their lives?

Part Four

Making the Transition

Chapter 12

Transformation

What then are the transformational elements that help the transitional size church grow into a larger congregation? The following elements are important.

Start with the End in Mind

When I work with the leadership of a transitional size congregation, I do not start by asking them to improve their strengths or deal with problem solving. I ask them simply, "How large can your church be?" I ask them to visualize the future and see a much larger congregation. I even ask them to pick the attendance number for this future church. This vision will include changes in the facility and adding programs and staff for this large community.

For example, a congregation with 175 ASA tells me that in three years they want to be at 350 ASA. I ask them to work backward from that number. What would it look like for them to reach this number? How many services would this involve? What other programs would need to be offered? What staff would need to be hired? Then we put together strategies to make this happen. The leadership starts with a very important transformational tool: start with the end in mind. This allows church leadership to see things that they cannot see now.

While teaching at a conference for transitional size churches, I had a wonderful opportunity to demonstrate the power of starting with the end in mind. I asked the leaders of one church if they would be willing to answer some questions in front of the other church leaders. I started by asking what they thought their church needed to do at the present time to grow. I listed their responses on newsprint for everyone to see.

After they had created this list, I asked the pastor what Easter attendance had been for the previous two years. I took the two numbers and found the average. It was right at 450. Then I asked the leaders to imagine their church having an average attendance of 450. I started by asking what Easter attendance would then be. They agreed on 800 for the number. I then said, "Imagine that three years from now your church will have 800 people for Easter and an average Sunday attendance of 450. What must you do right now to make that happen?"

This group now created a second list. They became very excited as they brainstormed ways to make this happen. The room was full of electricity as the rest of the conference saw this group's excitement. At the end of the exercise, I put the two different lists alongside each other. "What is the difference?" I asked the other participants.

There were a lot of answers, but the one that got everyone's nod of agreement was, "They had passion with the second list. You just knew they could do it!" Start with the end in mind! Too many congregations plod along making minor adjustments and fumbling with balancing budgets and fixing their air conditioning. The reason congregations have leaders is to lead. It helps if you know where you are going.

A Vision in Three Parts

The congregational leaders will need to create out of this vision three plans and begin to act on them. The first is a staffing plan. The second is a program plan. The third is a facilities plan. All three will be needed.

The Staffing Plan

The staffing plan aims at adding new staff. These must be staff who are capable of bringing in new families to help pay for their addition to the staff. This is important because not all staff positions will pay for themselves and not all individuals know how to find 20 new families in order to make this happen.

I ask congregations to avoid adding maintenance and support-staff positions. The church may need a part-time accountant to pay the church bills, but this position will not pay for itself. When forced to choose, I ask congregations to aim at developmental positions. Here are the ones that I find helpful for the transitional church:

- the youth pastor
- a competent Christian education or family ministry staff person
- a newcomer coordinator or lay ministries coordinator (these people function as the human resources managers of a congregation)
- a music minister. Note that I did not say an organist/choirmaster. A music minister creates new opportunities for the musical talents in a church.

Frequently, leaders of transitional size churches ask me how many new families they will need to add for every one of these positions added. This is the wrong question. Just as in business, churches have to capitalize on the future. The better question is, "How long will we have to pay for this position before we will be able to absorb this cost into our regular operating budget?" The answer to this question is 24 to 36 months, normally. This, however, is highly dependent on being able to find the right kind of staff person.

Take the youth pastor, for example. I have found many young people who would like to be full-time youth pastors. What these people want is to find a church with a large number of youth already in a youth group and a group of dedicated adults who are willing to work with this ministry. This is not the kind of youth pastor that a transitional size church needs.

A transitional size church needs a person who, during the interview, says something like, "I am excited about the challenge of building a youth ministry. I love working with kids and I especially like to get a group of adults to work with me on this. I have actually done exactly this kind of thing in another setting." One of the great truths in hiring people is "past performance is the best indicator of future behavior"! I especially like the energetic youth pastors who are willing to work full-time for half a salary until they have created ministries that will pay for their work.

What I am emphasizing here is the importance of the developmental nature of the position. This is very different from a staff person in a very large congregation in which maintaining momentum is more important than developing the ministry.

The Program Plan

Most transitional size churches have created some human felt need ministries. Usually these are understaffed and underdeveloped. Since resources are limited, the congregational leaders need to create a priority list of ministries to be funded and new ones to be started. A good place to start is by looking at the needs of present members. For example, a church in Florida made up of many older members wanted my help in building programs to attract younger people. I directed them to the needs of their older members. Once they began to create programs to support their own people, it was an easy step to extend this to others.

I do want to offer a caution here. Transitional size churches are vulnerable to new ideas. What do I mean by this? Just because there is a need out there does not mean that your congregation is called to meet it. There are many good ideas that want funding. This is not the same as a congregation's calling. I find that a congregation's calling is more directly related to the passion of the members. Many congregations have never taken the time to discover what their members really care about. Pastors often assume that members care passionately about what the pastor or the denomination cares about. This is often not true.

This means that a key ingredient of program planning is knowing the congregation's vision and passion. For Christians, *vision is a compelling picture of future events that have been guaranteed by the death and resurrection of Jesus Christ*. Passion is what the members of the congregation care deeply enough about to work, give, and sacrifice in order to make that vision happen.

The Facilities Plan

I will not say much about this part of the congregation's development except to note that this plan often gets the most attention. Interestingly, of the three plans, this is actually the easiest part to create. Most architects are trained in how to lead a group of leaders through a needs assessment process and then develop an architectural rendering to meet these needs. So the key here is to find the right architect.

Experience has taught me to pay attention to an item that is often left off a building plan. This is the total site plan. For example, many congregations place a new building in the center of their existing property. Once this is done, it limits the future development that can be placed on that site. This is why I like to see a master plan for the site before I see a particular building plan.

Besides these three plans, there are other ingredients that are needed for transformation and growth to occur.

Act Like a Large Church

Another key element is to start behaving like a large congregation. In seminars, I often take transitional church leaders on a tour of a growing 400 plus ASA congregation. I describe how the board functions. I describe the clergy's job in such places. I describe staff meetings and program options. I take these people on such a tour to offset the intuitive hunches that can lead them astray. Then I make suggestions based on this model.

If only one adult class is offered, create three more. (The pastor may have to give up teaching for a season to empower these options.) If a third service is needed for younger families, design a young-family service, staff for it, and offer it. Create a new way to pastor the congregation. Teach people this new pastoring method and reinforce it. Make this new pastoring method part of the greater system. A key element in all this is to increase the stewardship of the members. As we have seen, the larger church is more programmatic in its stewardship and receives larger average gifts from its members. It is extremely important to continually communicate why these things are being done. It is not "to get larger"; it is to serve people better and to carry out the great commission.

Sometimes I am asked how large I think a church should be. Although in one sense this is a very individual question and is based on a unique congregation, I have found over the years one answer that fits all congregations. "A church should be large enough to have the people and resources necessary to carry out the mission that God has given it."

Change the Pastor's Job Description

This means primarily pruning the activities that the pastor does that are not essential to this position. This takes courage on the part of the pastor, and support from the lay leaders. It is not easy to change behavior, but it is even harder when people keep reminding you of their small-church expectations.

The Transformational Leader

What Characteristics Does the Transformational Leader Have?

- A willingness to try the new
- The ability to change
- The ability to create a guiding coalition of key congregational leaders
- The ability to see today what will happen tomorrow
- The ability to create both a vision and a strategic plan
- The tenacity to persevere in the face of resistance and to give ideas the time and energy to work
- The ability to inspire others

Two Types of Leadership

As we have seen in this information on church size or culture, there are two types of leadership. There is the leader that takes a congregation that is small for its type and leads it to become a larger congregation, but still within its former size range. I call this kind of leadership the congruent kind. This is the pastor leading the pastoral size congregation by loving the people and giving his or her energy to reaching out and connecting to new people on a relationship basis. This is the key to bringing the existing system to health and vitality without changing the kind of congregation it already is.

I tell my friends in the ministry to avoid taking on the church with an ASA of 165, especially when following a well-liked pastor. In these situations, it is more predictable that, despite the sense that they are ready to grow, the congregation will decline. Better, I suggest, to take the congregation at 90 ASA that did not particularly care for the former pastor, or in which the previous pastorate was less than five years. Why? Because it is easier to grow a system *within* the system than beyond it.

A second type of leader takes a congregation beyond these boundaries. This I call transformational leadership. It takes unique skills to be this kind of pastor. (See the chart on page 111.) Can you learn these skills? I believe that many pastors can, but this is not easy. The main problem with learning to be a transformational leader is overcoming two dynamics. The first is knowing what worked for you in a smaller size church. The second is even more difficult, and it is habit.

Habit is both a powerful tool and a limiting dynamic. I am glad that each time I get into my car, I do not have to think about driving. I certainly hope I pay attention to the road, but I do not think much about coordinating the clutch and the gas pedal. It has become habit. We humans habitualize much of life.

Most pastors head off to the office Monday morning without thinking much about what they are doing. When we grow and change as leaders, we often become painfully self-aware of our behavior. We are grace-filled to remember that change takes time. It will take persistence to be a transformational leader and to take a transitional size congregation to another level.

If you want to learn more about becoming a transformational leader, I suggest that you read Robert Quinn's *Deep Change*. It is the best book that I have ever read on transformational leadership.

Let Those Who Need to Leave, Leave!

Some people will never be happy with the church's growth. They joined because they wanted the benefits of a small congregation. Some members become unhappy and some will threaten to leave. Now, let's be clear about this. It is not their leaving that is a problem; it is their staying and constantly resisting and spreading negativity. Some pastors act as though the worst thing in the world is to have some-one leave. Let me assure you it is not.

Over the years, I have had to face a demon that many other pastors have also had to face. I truly want people to like me. I hope that they will love me. Of course, I can rational-ize this by wrapping it around the great commandment of Jesus to "love one another." The hard truth to face, howev-er, is that this is not the reason that I want such love. Mostly, I want to find in the ministry the kind of unconditional love and acceptance that I often did not find in my family of ori-gin. I am tempted to believe that if I am good enough as a pastor—work hard enough, preach the best sermons, visit enough families—people will love me. It is, of course, a myth. It is also the source of much compulsive behavior and the need to achieve. Pastors are not exempt from this need even though we are about "the Lord's business."

It is critical to remember that as the pastor of a congre-gation, each of us is called to a leadership role. We can lead for the right reasons or for wrong reasons. But, whether we lead for right reasons are for wrong ones, not everyone will thank us. I have seen good and godly pastors scorned and rejected by congregations for doing all the right things. Doing all the right things does not guarantee that people will love us. Sometimes they do, sometimes they do not. Sometimes they choose to leave. When they do, bless them in their going.

Grow Quickly, Not Slowly

Finally, let me point out that it is also helpful to pursue plans that allow the congregation to make major steps for-ward. Incremental and slow change only keeps the congre-gation in this limbo state too long. People wear out, things fatigue, pastors move on. In his excellent book *44 Ways to Increase Church Attendance*, Lyle Schaller offers several activ-ities that are proved to increase your church's attendance. Settle on one or two of these and execute them. I suggest that transitional size churches add four to eight "Special Sundays" during the next year. (See the box below on how to put on a Special Sunday.)

Special Sundays

These must be compatible with the values, personality, and goals of your congregation. You are limited only by the imagination of those doing the planning. There are at least five areas that work for a special Sunday.

1. The recognition of special vocations or occupations: healthcare professionals (near St. Luke's Day), firemen, veterans, teachers, Scout leaders.

2. Special liturgical days: First Sunday of Lent, Good Friday, All Saints' Day, Pentecost, All Souls' Day. (Remember that the largest number of present parish members attend church on Palm Sunday.)

3. National holidays and other special days: Martin Luther King Jr.'s birthday, Veterans' Day, Father's Day, Mother's Day, World Hunger Day, and so forth.

4. Other special days in your church: The anniversary of the founding of the church, the patron saint day, mid-February marriage celebration, clergy ordination anniversary, long-time member recognition.

5. Community concerns: keeping kids safe, keeping kids off drugs, recovery Sunday, single parents Sunday, celebrating grandparents, and so forth.

As you can see, the possibilities are endless. However, just scheduling a special Sunday will do little.

How to Organize a Special Sunday

- Appoint a taskforce of five to seven people who genuinely care about the topic.

- Have the task force coordinate with the day's preacher and the musicians.

- Make a list of special people to invite.

- Announce this special day weeks in advance.

- In the weeks before, announce it often, and have prayers for the day.

- Encourage members to invite guests based on the day's theme.

- Consider a large, red, canvas banner to drop over your sign or church building advertising the event.

- Plan a possible follow-up event to connect further with attendees; for example, a Christian counselor to speak to blended families.

Trust me, the congregation will work better once it passes an ASA of 225! Create a season of growth, work hard at it, and persevere.

Questions

1. Which of these key elements of transformation do you believe your congregation needs to take on at this time?

2. Which of these elements will be the most difficult?

3. Is the pastor primarily a congruent leader or a transformational one?

Chapter 13

Hunching Your Way to the Promised Land

One reason that transitional size congregations find the transformation so difficult is because what works well for the pastoral size congregation does not work well for the program size congregation. When a transitional size congregation's leadership has to make this transition, the tendency is to intuitively hunch our way forward. The leaders then tend to rely on what is working best at the present time. They cannot see the counterintuitive things that make the larger church distinctive. They tend to think that a larger church is just their congregation with twice or three times as many people in it. This leads to two common mistakes.

"Expanding the Pastor"

If the pastoral size church grew because it had a healthy, emotionally present, and energetic pastor, then it seems logical to extend the next step of the church by "expanding the pastor." How can you do this? One very unproductive way is to keep expanding the responsibilities of the pastor until she or he burns out.

However, an even more common mistake is to believe that an additional pastor will automatically help the church grow. This person, often called the assistant or associate pastor, is expected to expand the pastoral role so that growth will be a natural consequence. Why does this seldom work?

First, although the senior pastor feels stressed and

genuinely believes that pastoral help is needed, the sources of this stress often have more to do with the senior pastor doing the wrong things and being unable to focus on the few things that are most essential to the pastor's role. Suppose that the senior pastor is a gifted preacher and teacher. The presence of a second pastor only means that the senior pastor will have less opportunity to teach or preach. It is probably not the amount of time teaching and preaching that is a drain on the senior pastor; it is probably the time spent in areas that do not have the same kind of vocational and psychic reward.

Second, the senior pastor must now supervise another pastor. This is a very different skill set from doing the work oneself. Often it is just easier to do something yourself than to teach another person to do it. The skills of supervision and staff development are very sophisticated and advanced skills. This also means being aware of another person's schedule and relationships within the parish. All this adds to the demands on the senior pastor, and does little to lighten the load.

Third, it is very easy for two pastors to divide the congregation's loyalty and this could lead to tension and even a congregational fight. I should mention that for many churches with an attendance nearing 200, a second pastor is more predictably a way to create two congregations rather than grow the original one.

Fourth, few pastors know how to find a person with complementary skills. Most find someone just like them (raising the potential for either redundancy or competition) or the complete opposite. Finding the complete opposite makes teamwork and communication very difficult.

Fifth, what the senior pastor really needs is not another pastor but more help in general, such as janitorial help, secretarial help, or administrative help. In the transitional size congregation, the pastor is often doing jobs that in the larger church are just given to other staff.

Sixth, in most denominations, a second pastor is too

expensive an addition at this stage of the congregation's life. The same position filled by a competent layperson is probably a third less expensive. It isn't that clergy are highly paid, but at the entry level, the added benefits are expensive.

Seventh, if the two pastors are from different generations, and if both are males, serious conflict often arises. It is a guy thing!

Extend the Board

Most effective pastoral size churches have developed a good working relationship between the pastor and the lay governing board. This team approach works well in this smaller size congregation. However, in a larger church, the board's task moves away from management and more toward oversight. It is natural, however, given the intense involvement of the board at the smaller level to believe that what the congregation really needs to grow is the board. Expanding the board is frequently done by creating committees.

I am often given a flowchart by clergy in the transitional size churches and asked what I think of it. You may remember my response to Bob. Now, I always answer, "It is a great chart. Did you do this in Excel or what?" Usually, they think for a while and then realize this isn't what they want to know. What they want to know is, "Will it work?"

The answer is yes and no. The plan may work for a while, but it usually will not work for long. Here is why. When the board generates a number of working committees or commissions, there is a surge in immediate energy and activity. This is because the board has created a new entity that needs new leaders. So, for the first few months, new leaders (often newer members) are asked to fill the committee slots. This broader involvement of newer people and the incorporation of new leaders lead to more effective assimilation. However, it does not take very long for this system to fatigue.

First, these committees and commissions usually expand

the maintenance structure of the congregation. This will lead to more complexity in relationships and in decision making. This makes the structure slower in responding to changing needs.

Second, while the increased number of committees and commissions increases the number of leaders who are stakeholders in the congregation, it does not increase the actual number of people involved in life-transformational ministries like changing diapers or leading people to Christ.

Third, and most important, within a year this system will need to be maintained. New members must be recruited to fill off-going slots and those of people who move away. At that point, the system begins to demand more and more maintenance from both the board and the pastor. In other words, the critical issue isn't "Will this work?" but "What if it does work?"

Both of these strategies reflect the system hunching its way along. The problem is that becoming a larger church involves transformation, not extension. It demands counter-intuitive information. What both the pastor and the board of a church with 150 ASA each Sunday would be surprised to discover if they looked at the healthy church with 350 ASA each Sunday is *how much the board and pastor of that larger church don't do!* This is something that we will look at in the next chapter.

Questions

1. What other intuitive mistakes could the small church make as it views the larger congregation?

2. How does the larger church deal differently with additional clergy staff?

Chapter 14

What the Large Church Knows

We have seen how smaller churches often make mistakes by hunching their way forward. They are trying to become large by doing what has worked so far. A better way forward is to take a look at healthy larger congregations with well-established program culture and see what they know that you don't. We can phrase it this way, "What skills has the program church learned that the transitional church must learn?" I have found seven essential skills.

A New Style of Organizing

The program church has learned that the church is not one group of people but a diverse community with several different congregations, ministries, and organizations. With this comes the basic assumption *that not everyone has to do everything!* The program church offers choices to people. Many of these choices are based on the felt needs of members and nonmembers. Communications from the congregation make it clear who may attend these events, but everyone knows that the choice is theirs.

The assumption of the pastoral size church is that adult education, the Lenten program, and the fall fair are for everybody. The communications assume that everyone knows this and the active members should attend.

Often in a larger congregation, the different worship services themselves function as a congregation within the larger congregation. I once worked with a congregation with an ASA of 1,250 people. Since their worship building only held around 400, the congregation offered a wide variety of services with varying styles, which included a 6 P.M. Saturday evening and 7:30 P.M. Sunday evening. Many members of that church identified most with the service they attended. "We attend the 4:30 Sunday afternoon traditional service," an older couple explained to me. Although people do visit other services, they usually see one as home.

Sometimes these "congregations" are identified as ministry areas. As we have seen, in a large church, the music ministry, the men's ministry, the women's Bible study, the young mother's group and the 12-Step recovery ministry can each become a place of identification and belonging.

In a way, the pastor and staff of the large church have learned that each of these congregations within the congregation needs attentiveness, will run through a life cycle, and must have someone who will shepherd the people in it. The good news is that each of these congregations becomes an additional point of entry for new people.

Another System for Pastoral Care

One of the great myths of the smaller congregation is that *if* they have a good pastor, the people receive good pastoral care. Conversely, large churches, they think, must be made up of impersonal numbers. In practice, this is much different.

The large church, with its myriad of felt need offerings, diverse staff, and reservoir of leaders, has much greater potential to offer specialized pastoral care and to deliver it more effectively. For example, the congregation that I served in Seattle not only had a Christian counseling center, we also had support groups for widows, single unmarried young professionals, those recovering from addiction, and even a specialized ministry to women who had been sexually abused as children. If the people in these groups had waited for my availability and even awareness in order to receive the care they needed, they would have had to wait a long time.

In the smaller congregation, pastoral care usually is the

pastor and this means that help is almost always one-on-one and limited to the knowledge and skills of the pastor. This also means that although the general issues of hospital visitation, premarital counseling, and grief support at the time of loss are being offered, the above specialties just are not there.

What are the options for such an alternative system? Here are a few suggestions:

- Trained lay visitors for hospital and nursing homes
- Trained counselors, sometimes called "lay pastors," for the range of general counseling situations
- A program such as the "Stephen Ministry" that both trains and oversees a lay visitation and counseling ministry
- Cell groups organized around age and other demographics with well-trained group coordinators
- Teaching leaders of ministries and organizations to be "co-pastors" with the senior pastor. This means asking each leader to commit to some form of pastoral oversight (a hospital visit when necessary) for each member
- Some combination of the above

Some congregations that have been large for many years have followed an older pattern of hiring more clergy staff as the congregation grows. This is largely not economically feasible in today's world. Some congregations have done this by having available a large number of retired clergy to help in pastoral care. However, the newer method of sharing this ministry with the baptized members of the church has proved to be more effective in almost every situation.

Staff to Meet the Future

No matter how large a congregation, financial resources are still difficult to manage. The large church has learned to use these funds wisely when it comes to staff. Most congregations use a wise balance of paid and unpaid staff members to manage the needs of the congregation. Without a doubt, a critical thing most large churches have learned is that when you hire staff, hire for the future and not the past.

When I first took on my job for the Episcopal Diocese of Texas, a clergyperson in a large church took me to lunch to discuss his church's various ministries. He was particularly excited by the fact that the leadership had "finally decided to take his advice" and hire a full-time administrator for the congregation. "I've been after them to do this for five years," he added with a sense of triumph. Later he asked me what I thought about that decision. I told him that I thought it was good that his church finally had been able to hire this administrator, but that I was troubled about what it may mean for the future. I asked him what position he would add today if he had the funds to do this. He explained immediately that he really needed to take on their effective part-time youth pastor into a full-time position.

"What do you think that this means?" he asked me.

"Congratulations," I responded. "You have just staffed your church for five years ago. I would have found a volunteer to administer things and hired the youth pastor."

I watched with interest the dawning recognition in his face. "Do you think it will take you five more years to get the youth pastor full-time?" I asked.

"No, not after this lunch," he said with a determined look that told me he was armed with the right information. Healthy large churches know the key developmental question is, Who is the next staff person we need to hire for the future?

Excellence in All We Do

The large congregation has learned a word that the small church almost never uses. It is the word *excellence*. The attitude is "if it is worth doing, it is worth doing with excellence." The reason for this has to do with the large percentage of new and marginal people in the larger church.

The large church knows that visitors and newcomers measure an offering from the congregation on the basis of quality, not relationship. This means that a drama program offered as part of the liturgy has to be done very well, with excellence. It is rehearsed professionally and will not be put on until it is ready. If it is badly done, visitors will be turned off by it. Nowhere is this truer than in the music and the preaching of a large congregation.

The small congregation has a different standard that is driven by the familiarity of members with one another. For example, the organist may not play very well (she hasn't figured out what those foot pedals are for on the organ) but she volunteered when we couldn't hire a replacement for our last organist. She is a dear soul and we are glad that she can offer this for us. She means well and we value her. Needless to say, these values have almost no meaning in a larger church.

This also becomes important in the quality of sermons. In the small church, the network of pastoral relationships gives the preacher a real advantage. People don't care if the pastor uses the fishing analogy one more time; after all, they know that it has been a busy week in the congregation. Again, this has no meaning for a larger church. A poor or redundant sermon preached in a large church risks losing the new and marginal people. In addition, the large-church pastor has learned that his or her 20 minutes in the pulpit are the only time for intimacy, support, pastoral care, and instruction for many in the church.

This leads to a strange paradox that I have often observed about the difference between preaching in some large churches versus small ones. I have found that many dynamic preachers in large congregations—Bill Hybels, for example—share much more vulnerable and personal sermons than many of their small-church counterparts. Part of the reason for this is the bind the small-church preacher feels about being vulnerable and sharing information that may seem to violate confidences in this small community.

A pastor such as Bill Hybels can say, "A troubled young couple came to see me recently when they were thinking about giving up on their marriage." By doing this, he can help the many struggling couples in his congregation. If this is said in a small church, the most significant reaction is people looking at the three young couples present that probably fall into this category and wondering who the pastor is talking about.

Can the preacher in a small church still share such intimate information? Yes, but she or he should learn that no matter when the event took place, in the sermon it should always be disguised with, "In my last congregation, I had a young couple come to see me."

A New Role for the "Nongeneric Organization or Ministry"

Small congregations have organizations that exist to maintain the small congregation or to represent the denomination's expectations. For example, almost every major denomination expects its congregations to have some sort of women's auxiliary. Often these provide support for denominational missionary work, and are organized around the needs of the denomination.

The large church has generated many organizations and ministries that are organized around the felt needs of people both in and outside the congregation. The large church becomes skilled at regularly asking, "What is out there, what hurt or need, that we need to touch?" Often, the congregational leaders research this, plan a well-organized response, and meet the need in effective ways. This response not only touches members where they hurt, it has the potential to touch nonmembers. These responses become entry points into the congregation.

Sometimes these responses to need can be quick and dramatic. In June 2000, Tropical Depression Allison dropped more than 25 inches of rain in a 48-hour period in the Houston area. Many areas of the city were flooded and many people were forced out of their homes. One pastor, Ed

Young, of Second Baptist Church, took dramatic action. He canceled all Sunday services but then asked members to come and prepare food packages and relief supplies for their hurting members. Not only did hundreds of members respond, but many others, Christian and non-Christian, came to help out.

This action got plenty of public press, and the pastor's face was seen on TV for several days following this event. He became the Christian spokesperson—*the* pastor—to the Houston community. Denominational leaders such as bishops, superintendents, and conference moderators were nowhere to be seen. This single event drove home to me the new role of the so-called "large pastoral church" of several thousand members in our society today.

Further, the pastors and staffs of larger congregations are constantly attending conferences where the best practices of other churches in meeting human need are being taught. This becomes an energizing pattern of ministry. The large church is constantly asking, "What do our people need?" and "What is out there in society that we can touch?" By asking this, and by having more of these kinds of ministries than those that simply maintain a congregation, the large church continues to grow.

A New Role for the Church Board

Whether it is called a vestry, session, board, or some other title, an elected body of elders governs most Protestant congregations. The role of this body changes dramatically as the size of a congregation increases.

In the smallest church, the family size congregation, the board is made up of the leaders of significant families. They are both leaders and workers. In the pastoral sized church, the board is a leadership council that shares with the pastor in the oversight of all of the congregation's life. The board and pastor have oversight and management responsibilities.

In the large church, it is no longer possible or desirable to have the governing board manage anything. For one reason, they are not there enough. For another, each member is most connected to the congregation within the congregation where he or she most often participates. The congregation becomes larger, but the staff now has more responsibility for the management of the church. The board now takes on a specialized ministry. What is this ministry? It is vision, policy, and oversight. Simply said, it is the *big* picture.

In the small church, a frequent challenge is found in what I call the incestuous relationships among board membership. What I mean is that it is hard for one to review the adult education program because the head of this program is married to a board member. The music person cannot be fired because she is the sister of a board member. In a small church, the challenge is overcoming the intimacy and relationships among the people that make management, especially accountability, difficult.

In the large church, the challenge goes the other way, and involves helping the board members see the large picture and getting them to appreciate the other congregations and ministries within the congregation.

A simple example of this is the issue of time. If a typical board meeting at a church with an ASA of 100 is two hours, do we really expect the large church with an ASA of 300 to have six-hour meetings? Well, we can joke that some do! But, the better way is to learn to delegate and avoid the temptation to micromanage the life of the congregation. Many large-church boards have learned that the following are important:

- Problems and issues should be discussed by some other appropriate group that recommends a course of action before the issues are brought before the whole board
- These items should be submitted in writing before the meeting

- The board needs time for vision and goal setting, which usually needs to be done at another time other than during the regular meeting
- Have more frequent board meetings lasting shorter amounts of time
- Clearly distinguish between the maintenance items of the agenda and those that involve oversight and policy
- Learn to trust others
- Discuss how decisions will be made and what procedures will be followed for voting (best done before an explosive item appears)
- Realize that most decisions made after 9 P.M. are usually bad ones
- Long-range planning is best done by a specially appointed visionary group who report to the board
- Facilities are always managed better by people than by committees

Sensitivity to the Seeker in Everything

The large congregation knows that as many as 20 percent of those attending worship may not be members of either the congregation or the denomination. This makes the large church much more sensitive to the presence of seekers. Given this sensitivity, communications, publications, and announcements guard against denominational or Christian "in" language.

The large church has learned that "general announcements" on Sunday are very ineffective forms of communication. A good rule of thumb that many large congregations have learned is, "Does this announcement directly affect those worshiping at this service?" If not, drop it. Communications to church organizations and ministries are done in specific ways and aimed only at those affected.

In addition, many large churches have learned the value of using music that is more culturally acceptable to younger adults. They have learned that depression is a more important topic for a sermon than whether ravens literally delivered food to Elijah. Further, they have learned that joy is a better topic than rules, love is better than anger, and that being a committed person is better than being a member of the denomination. They learned all this from their seekers.

They have also learned that we live in a visual culture surrounded by TVs, computers, and movies, and that the average American hasn't read a book in two years. They have learned that solemn, sober, and heavy European classical music has a very select market and that vibrant, uplifting music of any kind with strong percussion support can be found on most successful radio stations.

Most of all, they have learned that people in American society think that choice is a good thing and that membership is not a destination for most people.

The small but growing congregation will want to ask if they are prepared to learn the lessons that large congregations have paid the price to learn.

Questions

1. Which of these seven elements of a large church does your congregation already know?

2. Which ones do your congregation need to learn?

3. What expectations concerning *excellence* do you already have?

4. What percentage of your congregation's life rests in the large church and what percentage is still within the small church?

Chapter 15

What Is Your Next Step?

When I work with transitional congregations, I constantly focus the leadership on their most important next step, the step that they can take to most leverage the future development of the congregation.

For many transitional congregations, the next step is to share the information in this book with the general membership. This helps ease tension and facilitate change when the change begins to generate resistance.

For some pastors, the next step is to realistically assess the congregation's real abilities to transition into a larger and different congregation. Along with this, the pastor must realistically assess his or her own leadership abilities by asking if he or she is willing to change his or her style of ministry to become a transformational leader.

A key step in moving in this direction is to find a mentor who has led this kind of change. It is hard to become what you cannot see. This person may not be easy to find. This is not necessarily the pastor of a larger church, because this pastor may be just leading a congregation congruent with its large culture.

As I began working more and more with congregations and their pastors, I found that transitional size congregations presented a unique set of challenges. I found a great deal of congregations out there who talked about growing churches, even speaking of "the church growth pastor." Out of my own experience, however, something did not seem right.

Eventually, I discovered two elements that helped me be of help to others. First is to understand churches as systems and not merely organizations. This view is presented in this book. The second, and more powerful element, was to interview pastors who had broken the mythological 200 Barrier. There actually are not too many of these churches and there certainly were not many in my denomination. When I interviewed these pastors, I did not hear the predictable stories about programs or cell groups. What I heard was a story about inner frustration that led to change. All these pastors told me a personal transformation story.

In his important book, *Deep Change*, Robert Quinn talks about the relationship between the leader's own life and the life of the organization. He states that only leaders who are willing to do the hard work of deep change can lead their congregations through this change. He is right.

That is why I have told this story through the lives of pastors like Bob and Ted. These are real people and their stories are real. The story is about systems and leaders, or in scriptural language, it is about the Body of Christ and its gifted leaders.

I hope this book has given you insight. I hope that I have given you tools for the journey. But, above all, I hope that I have given you encouragement. There was a time when being a pastor was a privilege with a lot of cultural perks, and that being a member of a congregation was customary. Today, the role of pastor is stressful and no one *has* to be a member of a church.

We have become, in the United States, a missionary church in an increasingly secular society. I see no chance of this trend reversing itself. The road ahead will be hard. If we see the re-Christianization of North America, it will happen in the lives of local believers who struggle with the great commission in our own day. This means it will happen in congregations, small ones and large ones.

There is, of course, nothing virtuous about size. I have seen vibrant small churches and sick large ones. What is true is that none of us who follow Christ have been exempted from the great commission. May God grant you strength and the guidance of his Holy Spirit as you commit yourself to the important task of bringing those who know not Christ into a relationship with him and with the community that is called by his name.

Suggested Reading List

This is a selection of books and journals I have found helpful and have recommended to those who are interested in the topic of leadership for congregations in the twenty-first century.

Leadership

Anderson, Leith. *Dying for Change*. Minneapolis: Bethany House, 1990.

Bennis, Warren. *Leaders: Strategies for Taking Charge*. New York: HarperBusiness, 1997.

Callahan, Kennon L. *Effective Church Leadership: Building on the Twelve Keys*. San Francisco: Harper & Row, 1990.

Drucker, Peter F. *The Effective Executive*. New York: HarperBusiness, 1967.

Gangel, Kenneth O. *Feeding and Leading*. Wheaton, Ill.: Victor, 1989.

George, Carl F., and Robert E. Logan. *Leading and Managing Your Church*. Old Tappan, N.J.: F. H. Revell, 1987.

Schaller, Lyle E. *The Pastor and the People*. Rev. ed. Nashville: Abingdon, 1986.

Steinke, Peter L. *Healthy Congregations: A Systems Approach*. Bethesda, Md.: Alban Institute, 1996.

Organizational Development

Bridges, William. *Managing Transitions: Making the Most of Change*. 2nd ed. Cambridge, Mass.: Perseus, 2003.

Callahan, Kennon L. *Twelve Keys to an Effective Church*. San Francisco: Jossey-Bass, 1997.

Drucker, Peter. *Managing the Non-Profit Organization: Practices and Principles*. New York: HarperCollins, 1990.

Gladwell, Malcolm. *The Tipping Point*. Boston: Little, Brown, 2000.

Hanchey, Howard. *From Survival to Celebration: Leadership for the Confident Church*. Cambridge, Mass.: Cowley, 1994.

Payne, Claude E. *Reclaiming the Great Commission: A Practical Model for Transforming Denominations and Congregations.* San Francisco: Jossey-Bass, 2000.

Quinn, Robert. *Deep Change.* San Francisco: Jossey-Bass, 1996.

Rogers, Everett M. *Diffusion of Innovations.* 5th ed. New York: Free Press, 1995.

Rothauge, Arlin. *Sizing Up a Congregation for New Member Ministry.* New York: Episcopal Church Center, 1983.

Schaef, Anne Wilson, and Diane Fassel. *The Addictive Organization.* San Francisco: Harper & Row, 1988.

Schaller, Lyle E. *Parish Planning.* Nashville, Abingdon, 1971.

———. *Growing Plans.* Nashville: Abingdon, 1983.

———. *Looking in the Mirror: Self-appraisal in the Local Church.* Nashville: Abingdon, 1984.

———. *44 Ways to Increase Church Attendance.* Nashville: Abingdon, 1988.

———. *Create Your Own Future!* Nashville: Abingdon, 1991.

———. *The Seven-Day-a-Week Church.* Nashville: Abingdon, 1992.

———. *The Interventionist.* Nashville: Abingdon, 1997.

———. *Discontinuity and Hope: Radical Change and the Path to the Future.* Nashville: Abingdon, 1999.

Steinke, Peter L. *How Your Church Family Works: Understanding Congregations as Emotional Systems.* Washington, D.C.: Alban Institute, 1993.

Culture and Church

Anderson, Leith. *A Church for the 21st Century.* Minneapolis: Bethany House, 1992.

Hunter, George G. *Church for the Unchurched.* Nashville: Abingdon, 1996.

———. *The Celtic Way of Evangelism: How Christianity Can Reach the West ... Again.* Nashville: Abingdon, 2000.

Mead, Loren B. *The Once and Future Church Collection,* updated and rev. Bethesda, Md.: Alban Institute, 2001.

Sample, Tex. *U.S. Lifestyles and Mainline Churches: A Key to Reaching People in the 90's.* Louisville: Westminster/John Knox, 1990.

Schaller, Lyle E. *It's a Different World! The Challenge for Today's Pastor.* Nashville: Abingdon, 1987.